the joy of

home brewing
kombucha

HOW TO CRAFT PROBIOTIC AND FERMENTED DRINKS

Chad Turner

Skyhorse Publishing

Skyhorse Publishing books may be purchased in bulk at special discounts for sales promotion, corporate gifts, fund-raising, or educational purposes. Special editions can also be created to specifications. For details, contact the Special Sales Department, Skyhorse Publishing, 307 West 36th Street, 11th Floor, New York, NY 10018 or info@skyhorsepublishing.com.

Skyhorse® and Skyhorse Publishing® are registered trademarks of Skyhorse Publishing, Inc.®, a Delaware corporation.

Visit our website at www.skyhorsepublishing.com.

10 9 8 7 6 5 4 3 2 1

Library of Congress Cataloging-in-Publication Data is available on file.

Cover design by Mona Lin
Cover photo credit Getty images/iStock

Print ISBN: 978-1-5107-4610-7
Ebook ISBN: 978-1-5107-4611-4

Printed in China

This book is dedicated to Alicia Dimitrova: without your love, friendship, motivation, support, patience, advising, and understanding, this book wouldn't have been possible. I appreciate you more than you may ever realize.

CONTENTS

Introduction

I HEARD THE WORD *KOMBUCHA* for the first time in 2005. I was studying sustainable farming and ethno-botany in Costa Rica, where I was surrounded by an eccentric and eclectic group of green-living enthusiasts interested in such reverie as healthy eating, organic farming, and environmental protection. The location was a lush permaculture farm nestled in the wild jungle of the Caribbean coastline. The farm was superabundant with medicinal plants, native herbs, and fruit trees. When the trees bloomed, they dripped with exotic fruits and strange species that I had never seen in North America.

The cohabitants of the farm came in two categories: local Costa Ricans who had lived off the bounty of the jungle and ocean their entire lives, and North American and European travelers and students who were eager to get back to the land and investigate the transformative powers of local plants. One of the more well-read, experimental, and interesting of the eco-village residents was a French herbalist and cacao farmer named Tristan. Tristan had an infectious and bubbly personality and was always disappearing into the feral jungle or beach returning with mysterious roots, leaves, barks, mushrooms, and seeds of which he brewed into intriguing teas, tonics, and elixirs. One day, Tristan shared with me a sparkling tea-like concoction that he reported enhanced digestion, purified the liver, and balanced the body's pH. He said it was a Chinese mushroom tea called "kombucha." As he smiled with excitement, he explained, "It detoxifies our entire body and fights cancer, and it tastes like champagne." Beaming with life and enthusiasm, Tristan would hold up mason jars full of a deep, golden liquid that resembled an over-brewed batch of sun-tea. It appeared effervescent, containing fizzy, floating bubbles and unidentified particulates that resembled a dismembered jellyfish. I don't know if it was his embodiment of glowing health and infectious enthusiasm or the health claims he made about its capabilities, but my curiosity was seriously piqued, and I reluctantly took a sip.

It was tart, slightly sweet, and effervescent. It reminded me of sparkling apple cider that was mildly vinegary. I suspected there was something floral in it, but I couldn't put my finger on it. I didn't consider myself to have a very cultivated palate, but I found myself suddenly deconstructing the tart beverage like a sommelier. Ginger? Granny Smith apples? It was tingly and thirst-quenching and refreshing. It had the characteristics of a soda without the sickly syrupy sweetness. The flavors were definitely unique, and they reminded me of the many times I had consumed something that confused and arrested my taste buds: sour beer, vinegar, strong medicinal herbal teas. At the time, I hadn't had a beer in months and the slightly carbonated texture and amber color felt refreshing and comforting. I went in for another sip. And then another.

I continued to sip with curiosity and amusement. I felt the mood-elevating properties and its energizing effects almost immediately. Was it a placebo? Was it Tristan's vivacious and sprightly disposition that was allowing me to get caught up in the instantaneous feeling of the life-changing qualities of this libation? My quest for answers to nutritional queries and fermentation science would later reveal to me that well-brewed kombucha is high in a spectrum of B vitamins, playing a major role in energy synthesis and neurological function. My curiosity continued to grow.

I enjoyed my experience drinking kombucha in the rainforest of Costa Rica, and I quickly went in search of the energizing elixir upon returning to the United States. At the time of my return in 2006, the beverage was gaining popularity and I noticed large drink coolers in my local health-food stores devoted to kombucha primarily and a few other probiotic drinks that were beginning to gain traction. Attractive glass bottles with eye-catching labels listed the health benefits of the ancient elixir inside. They seemed to pop up overnight. What struck me was that these new healthy beverage display cases were strikingly similar to the soft drink and beer coolers in convenient stores and gas stations that dominated the American landscape.

The similarity of the coolers and of the carbonated beverages they showcased forced me to reflect on what the media and current public health climate had been referring to as America's "health crisis." Diabetes, heart disease, tooth decay, kidney failure, mineral depletion, and obesity among both adults and children was on the rise, and nearly every day there was a news story discussing the current health epidemic. One of the reported culprits of the health crisis was excess calories and chemical exposure of sugary soft drinks that could be purchased at every fast-food restaurant and convenience store. They weren't served in modest sizes fit for someone enjoying a guilty-pleasure snack. These calorie-dense refreshments of health-depleting properties were served in jumbo sizes. Liters, 20-ounce, 40-ounce, and even 64-ounce (just the thought makes me have to go to the bathroom) sizes were the norm and they were everywhere. Beverage coolers in gas stations, convenient stores, and supermarkets carried an exhausting variety of these unnaturally colored refreshments loaded with high-fructose corn syrup, artificial colors, endocrine disrupters, chemical preservatives, and synthetic stimulants. These were the beverages that health professionals had been attributing to the United States health crisis and obesity epidemic. I even questioned if these commentators and news reporters could fairly call this time in our history an "epidemic." Ebola, bubonic plague, cholera, Asian flu, and typhus fever are historical health epidemics. They are hard to avoid and deadly. Was it scientifically sound and justifiable to label the state of American's health an epidemic?

As I stood in front of the beverage display cases at my health-food store deciding which exotic flavor kombucha I was going to purchase, I was forced to ask myself: "Are probiotic drinks the answer to North America's health epidemic?" Were people now able to enjoy bottled fizzy libations similar to alcohol and sugary soft drinks, but with physical- and mental-health promoting properties instead of health-depleting properties? I was beginning to see hope for desperate Americans with self-destructive dietary habits and chronically bankrupt health. Then, as I reached for my flavor of choice, I became glaringly aware of the alarming price tag. Bottled kombucha and other fizzy probiotic drinks were valued at a premium level. At the time, most of the varieties were priced between $4 and $6 per bottle. The sticker shock is what made me realize that if I was going to enjoy the daily health benefits of this magical beverage and share its healing properties with the world, I needed to find a way to brew this wonder drink at home for less . . . much less.

I ordered a culture online and got to work making my first batch of home-brewed kombucha. This was my first exposure to the magical powers, and exploratory process, of fermentation, or so I thought.

I am a descendent of German and Polish immigrants. The south side of Milwaukee, Wisconsin, where I grew up has deep German and Polish roots. Fermented cabbage—sauerkraut—graced our dinner table on a regular basis. It was an important accompaniment to many meals as well as family and social gatherings. Our next-door neighbor of Polish descent fermented crocks of her own sauerkraut in her garage.

The most common fermented preparation in my hometown that made itself evident to me at an impressionable age was malted barley, hops, and yeast alchemy: beer. Milwaukee is widely known as "Beer City." German-bred Milwaukee was the hometown of many famous breweries including Miller, Blatz, Pabst Blue Ribbon, Shlitz, and Sprecher. So, I was no stranger to fermentation. It was deeply engrained in my cultural heritage and ethnic identity. It was all around me. Fermentation was responsible for many of my food habits, my connection to people and places, and was the very thing that brought my friends and family together.

At the time of my kombucha discovery, Costa Rica was the third country I had visited. My time working on a permaculture farm awakened a dormant curiosity of international travel and ethnobotany deep inside of me. It inspired my fascination with medicinal plants, superfoods, herbs, tonics, elixirs, teas, and health drinks. Furthermore, it developed my interest in how these traditional medicines are woven into the fabric of different cultures. I began my quest exploring the traditional knowledge and customs of people all over the world concerning plants and their medical, religious, and other uses. Fermentation and probiotic drinks became a major part of this quest. This fascination guided me to India to learn about Ayurvedic medicine and to study yoga. My search for medicinal teas and the origins of kombucha led me to the mountains and lowlands of China, where the first historical records of fermentation were found. This steered me toward traditional Chinese herbology, and the mind-body practices of ancient Chinese martial arts. At the time of writing this book, I have traveled to twenty-five countries exploring regional foods, languages, medicinal plants, local fermentations, and the synergistic way these all play a part in the health and identity of a culture and a region.

Since I met Tristan fourteen years ago, my experimentation and fascination has never stopped. Bubbling jars and crocks have become permanent fixtures and features in my kitchen, sometimes to the dismay of my family and previous housemates. Some of the recipes you will find in this book will be ready in days and others in weeks.

It's important to note that I was drawn to the world of fermentation to address my own health challenges. I was born with a neurological condition that runs in my family called narcolepsy, which affects my control of sleep and wakefulness, causing excessive daytime sleepiness. In some individuals, it can cause sudden uncontrollable sleep attacks. The interesting thing about narcolepsy is that, under western medicine, it is considered a neurological disorder and is treated with stimulants. Under many forms of alternative medicine, it is considered a digestive disorder. One method for treating narcolepsy and increasing the body's production of the alertness and wakefulness hormone, orexin, is by incorporating probiotics and fermented foods into the diet. Consuming fermented drinks, mainly kombucha, has greatly improved the quality of my and my family's lives. Needless to say, this book is very personal and an honor to write.

Well-known anthropologist Margaret Mead famously wrote "Food is for gifting," meaning that there is something more symbolic than just nutrition. Food and drink are meant to be exchanged and shared among family and friends. Consider this book a gift of health as well as a small contribution to the fermentation revival. A revival of ancient foods for the modern gut. This book was also written in defense of bacteria, which has been given a bad rap and have been under attack by uninformed doctors, antibacterial hand soaps, hand sanitizers, antibiotics, chlorinated tap water, and pesticides.

This book is the solution to those who would like to be sipping health-reviving kombucha every day but previously thought they couldn't afford to. *The Joy of Home Brewing Kombucha* is a book that shows you how to create healthy nonalcoholic fermented drinks for you and your family right in your kitchen using minimal equipment and ingredients. The recipes are designed to be easy to follow and are organized by popular drink categories. Nourish the bounty of friendly organisms that exist in these recipes so that they can, in turn, nourish you. You and your family will always have access to healthy and affordable nonalcoholic fermented drinks to sip on and enjoy. *The Joy of Home Brewing Kombucha* is full of nutritional DIY kitchen projects for all your favorite fermented drinks. As a health-conscious culinary enthusiast, you will now be armed with basic skills and encouraged to experiment with nutritious ferments in your own kitchen. Cheers to your health!

Disclaimer:
I am not a doctor, and the information in this book is not meant to be a substitute for professional medical care or advice. Some members of the medical and scientific community don't believe in the information written in these pages. Listen to your body, do your own research, experiment, and remember that not everything works for every person. It is imperative that I emphasize that kombucha and fermented drinks are not a cure for narcolepsy or any other specific disease, but they certainly may help. If you are suffering from any ailment whatsoever, it is strongly suggested you see a qualified, licensed medical professional. Throughout the years, I have worked at a variety of wellness centers, fitness clubs, yoga studios, chiropractic clinics, and health-food stores, and I have seen the transformative powers of probiotic drinks in myself and other people.

CHAPTER 1

A Brief History of Fermentation and Kombucha, and the Health Benefits of Probiotic Drinks

"Fermented foods may be the slowest and oldest fast food. The main ingredients in fermenting are your desire to play and time to wait. Some curiosity, a bit of optimism and an ability embrace naivety helps too."
—Sharon Flynn, author of *Ferment for Good: Ancient Foods for the Modern Gut*

MAKING PROBIOTIC-RICH FERMENTED DRINKS AND foods is not a revolutionary concept. Cultures around the world have been making fermented foods for health and longevity for thousands of years. Fermentation is the oldest form of food preservation, and it has numerous health benefits that go beyond preventing food from spoiling. Evidence exists of people fermenting drinks from all parts of the world as early as 7000 BC. The fermented probiotic drinks in this book and the ones found in your health-food store seem like a contemporary phenomenon, but the truth is that we know people consumed them in multiple different ancient cultures. Evidence can be found in sacred historical books such as the Bible and ancient Hindu texts.

The oldest documented fermented beverage was recorded in 7000 BC from a Neolithic village in the Henan Province of China. It was a wine-like fermentation brewed from rice, honey, Hawthorne fruit, and grapes. For the next few thousand years, many ancient cultures all over the world continued making a variety of different fermented drinks. Archeologists found evidence that Egyptians made wine from herbs, grapes, and tree resin. There are further findings that Egyptians wrote down thousands of herbal prescriptions and therapeutic cocktails that used fermented drinks as dispensing agents. The Incas of the Andes mountains crafted a beer-like fermentation made from corn and human saliva called Chicha. In Mesoamerica, currently modern-day Honduras, people brewed a "chocolate" wine from fermenting the sacred cacao plant. The ancient Nordics made a complex hybrid fermentation called Grog in which cereal grains were fermented and steeped with cranberries, lingonberries, and honey. This concoction was further infused with herbs such as bog myrtle, yarrow, juniper, and birch tree resin.

Many of these ancient fermented drinks had elevated alcohol content that prevented illness and infections by killing bacteria and parasites in contaminated water. A secondary benefit of alcoholic ferments was that they served as pain relievers and muscle relaxants. Alcohol could dissolve compounds that water couldn't, which allowed ancient brewers to experiment with more health-promoting additives such as leaves, roots, barks, berries, nectars, honey, tree saps, and resins. During fermentation, yeast and bacteria breaks down ingredients into easily digestible nutrients that the body can absorb quicker and easier. These original fermentations were designed to administer the nutritional properties of plants. Ancient medicines were delivered by way of fermented beverages.

In his book *The Barbarians's Beverage: A History of Beer in Ancient Europe*, fermentation historian Max Nelson discusses the many medicinal forms of early fermentations that resembled beer. Various fruits, plants, and even crushed up earthworms were put into beer for medicinal reasons. He reports that beer with crushed garlic was consumed for poisonous bites and beer drank warm with salt was a remedy against coughs. Cultures all over the world crafted their own versions of beer-like ferments, but they were far from the pasteurized pale filtered Budweiser people guzzle today. In fact, it's probably unfair for me to use terms like *wine*, *beer*, or *alcohol* because they are modern terms referring to libations that people enjoy now for different reasons and with very different recipes. Ancient fermentations were dispensing agents, a medium for delivering herbal medicines.

This book is about nonalcoholic, fermented probiotic drinks. None of the recipes included resemble what we think of as modern beer or wine, but similarly, they contain nutrition and health properties administered through fermentation. It is important to note that alcohol is a natural by-product of fermentation, and nearly all of the things in this book will create a small amount of alcohol as a natural part of fermentation. Most of them will have less than 1 percent alcohol when mature.

Food Preservation

Fermentation organisms produce alcohol, lactic acid, and acetic acid, all of which are natural biological preservatives sometimes referred to as *bio-preservatives*. Fermentation was used before refrigeration to make food shelf-stable and more digestible and to increase nutritional properties. In every region of the world I've visited, I have found a fermented food or drink with historical and cultural significance specific to that area. These ferments are distinctive and individual to the climate, seasons, fruits and/or vegetables, and unique colonies of bacteria of that biological region. Many of them were created for the sake of preservation and making food shelf-stable for longer. Others were invented to create an intricate and distinct flavor. Regardless of the primary reason for the initial fermentation, people enjoyed the energizing and digestion-enhancing health benefits as a secondary feature.

One of the most famous stories that highlight the food preserving powers and nutritional benefits of fermented foods comes from England in the 1760s. The East Indian Trading Company was experimenting with various potential cures for the terrible vitamin C deficiency disease known as scurvy, which was devastating to sailors and claimed the lives of many crewmen during the age of discovery. When Captain James Cook of the East Indian Trading Company left England for the South Pacific in 1768, he brought nearly 8,000 pounds of sauerkraut, a fermented cabbage with lactic acid bacteria, on board his ships to prevent scurvy. As a result, Captain Cook is credited with solving the scurvy conundrum and highlighting the vitamin-C-rich nutritional benefits of fermented foods. From that point forward, some variety of fermented foods were carried on English ships.

Legend also has it that Captain Cook landed upon the Polynesian Islands and was struck by how healthy the people were. He learned that a nutritious staple for Hawaiians and Polynesians throughout the Pacific was a fermented porridge made of yarrow and water called *poi*. All over the world, cultures have different

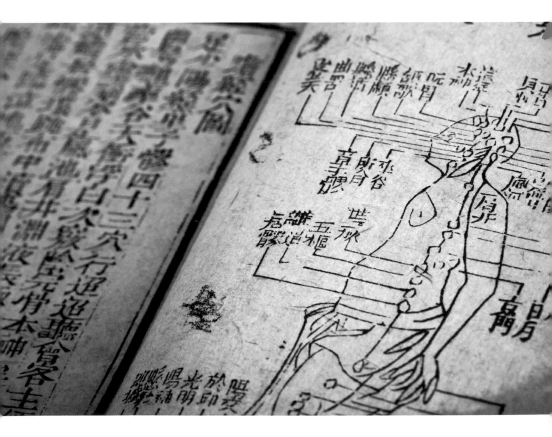

fermentations that have enhanced their health and slowly creeped into our modern-day grocery stores and condiment shelves. Korea gave us the delicious and complex flavors of kimchi. Russia is credited for kvass and kefir. Japan, for pickles and miso. China began fermenting black soy beans thousands of years ago, which is significant in a number of flavors and textures that we now enjoy for their health benefits in Asian cuisine. This list could go on and on. This book's major focus is on kombucha, which is believed to come from China or one of the countries nearby.

The History of Kombucha

Similar to kombucha, historic ferments were vehicles to administer the medicinal and nutritional benefits of the tea plant into our bodies while enjoying the digestive and longevity benefits of its probiotic nature.

There are many different stories about where kombucha came from. Historical records report it has been used in Eastern Europe, Russia, Japan, and China for many centuries. Some report that the first recorded use of kombucha comes from China during the Tsin Dynasty. In ancient China, fungi was considered to have magical properties, especially considering immortality. As Taoist philosopher James Roche states in his article "The History and Spread of Kombucha," kombucha was believed to be a fermented fungus tea before scientific exploration in the 1950s discovered that it was not a single organism but a symbiotic colony of bacteria and yeast with highly complex and sophisticated metabolic pathways. Other stories report that the name is Japanese. "Kombu" in Japanese refers to a type of seaweed, and "cha" is the word for tea. Another popular account reports that a Korean physician named Kombu treated the digestive disorders of Japanese Emperor Inyko with the fermented tea, and it was so successful that it was named "Kombu" and "cha" after him. By way of extended trade routes dating back to the silk road and the age of discovery, fermented teas made their way to Russia and Eastern Europe, where they were revered and enjoyed for their health benefits. Drinking fermented tea became quite popular in countries such as Germany, Italy, and England until food rationings during World War II created a shortage of two essential ingredients: tea and sugar.

Many different books and internet sites present various stories about the origins and history of kombucha. Some share similarities while others seem far-flung. As Sharon Flynn shares in her book *Ferment for Good: Ancient Foods for the Modern Gut*, there's not really a reliable source that speaks of the origin of kombucha. Like much throughout history, the stories are quite vague, and they've been around a long time. Flynn says, "It seems to come from Asia where there is a long history with tea."

Kombucha is the primary focus of this book and arguably the most popular home ferment and aforementioned store-bought probiotic drink. Kombucha gained substantial attention in the United States in the 1990s after the publication of Gunther Frank's book *Kombucha: Health Beverage and Natural Remedy from the Far East, Its Correct Preparation and Use.* In his book, Frank explains the ancient traditions, health benefits, and, as the title explains, proper preparation methods of kombucha. Around this same time, Americans suffering from terminal illnesses began consuming kombucha to boost their immune system and overall energy. In the late 1990s, GT's Kombucha, now the world's largest kombucha company, began brewing and bottling a variety of kombuchas using different teas, infusions, and fruit juices. The kombucha revival hit a new height when different varieties of GT's Kombucha made it onto the shelves of Whole Foods, the American upscale natural-food store. Kombucha once again became a common and easily enjoyed fermented tea, but this time it was being purchased instead of brewed at home as it had been before the rationing of World War II. GT's success and the widely known health benefits of kombucha came in part as the owner's mother reported consuming kombucha during her cancer treatment. This story is a strong part of the business's sales and marketing and outreach. More can be found at www.gts.livingfoods.com.

Today, the kombucha business in the United States generates millions of dollars per year. The different producers of kombucha now have their own trade organization and advocacy group,

Kombucha Brewers International. I wrote a large portion of this book while traveling across southeast Asia, and I noticed multiple varieties of kombucha sold in my local health foods stores were also available in places like Singapore and Hong Kong. This goes to show the revival and global outreach of this ancient health tonic.

Health Benefits of Kombucha

1. Hydrating, mineral rich, and thirst quenching. Better for you than soda, bottled juices, or sugary sports drinks.

2. Beneficial for gut biome. A happy digestive tract equals good physical and mental health.

3. Naturally rich in vitamins, minerals, probiotics, amino acids, polyphenols, and antioxidants.

4. Effective for treating various disorders, diseases, and infections. It brings body ecology back into harmony. Cures digestive disorders, increases energy, rebalances imbalances from overgrowth (or undergrowth) of candida, vaginal yeast infections, ulcers, constipation, and "undigested food."

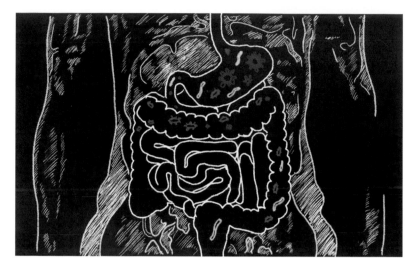

WHAT ARE PROBIOTICS?

Probiotics is the name for ingested bacteria. It is common for people to offhandedly refer to all bacteria and microorganisms in the
human body as probiotics, but truthfully, probiotics are only those
that we ingest. So the beverages in this book are probiotic drinks.
Microbiome, flora, micro-flora, beneficial microorganisms, and *gut
microorganisms* are some of the many terms and phrases used interchangeably for the colonies of friendly bacteria in the microscopic
world of our bodies. As you read this book and its many recipes, you
may see these words used interchangeably.

Probiotics are good bacteria that help promote and maintain a
healthy biome of intestinal flora. A healthy and balanced gut biome is
what we need to achieve digestive health, energy, nutrition absorption,
stable mental health, and alertness. Thousands of varieties of friendly
bacteria and yeast make up a healthy gut. The one strain believed to
be the most beneficial is *Lactobacillius*, which is the live culture found
in home ferments such as kombucha, kefir, and lacto-fermented sodas
and teas. Probiotics help maintain a balance of friendly-to-unfriendly
bacteria and keep our body's ecosystem in balance.

This is a culinary book designed to cultivate dense and diverse
microbial communities that you will drink so they can interact with
your gut microbiome. These interactions can improve digestion,
immune function, mental health, and other aspects of our well-
being. By eating a wide variety of probiotic, live-fermented foods,

you promote microbial diversity in your digestive tract. With our diet (including consumption of probiotic foods) and lifestyle, we as humans are aiming to maintain *symbiosis* or balance. If we become deficient in the necessary quantity and diversity of friendly gut bacteria, we create *dysbiosis* or imbalance.

The following are a list of common symptoms of imbalances in the body discussed in *The Probiotic Cure* by Martie Whittekin:

- Acne, skin eruptions, and foot problems
- Allergies and food sensitivities
- Halitosis and problems with your gums
- Chronic and unexplained fatigue
- Constipation, diarrhea, and other digestive problems
- Frequent infections including colds and flu
- Headaches
- Joint pain and inflammation
- Menopause symptoms
- Trouble sleeping
- Ulcers
- Unwanted weight gain
- Yeast overgrowth

The area of connecting health and digestion to bacteria began in 1908 when Russian biologist Dr. Ilya Metchnikoff earned a Nobel prize in medicine for discovering the microscopic world of our gut biome. He is considered the father of probiotics, because he identified the bacterial strains *Lactobacillus bulgaricus* and *Streptococcus thermophilus* and he concluded that they were beneficial and protective to our health. Metchnikoff believed that the key to longevity was a healthy diet and the daily consumption of fermented milk. He lived to the age of seventy-one in a time when the average life expectancy in France was not much more than forty.

Metchnikoff's discovery led us to understand that there is a zoo in our gut—a menagerie of micro-flora that require being fed and are sensitive to the quality and conditions of their environment or "terrain." Like all living things, probiotics need the right environment and nourishment to be "fruitful and multiply." His discovery further highlighted that each of us should think of ourselves as farmers and cultivators who are growing and developing colonies of health-promoting friendly bacteria. These bacteria are there to help fight off sickness and diseases. Our ability to digest food, maintain a healthy immune system, and ward off disease depend on the healthy terrain we have created in our digestive tract. Terrain is incredibly important for our health.

The World Health Organization defines probiotics as "live microorganisms that, when administered in adequate amounts, confer a health benefit on the host." To many people, the terms *friendly bacteria* or *beneficial microbes* sound contradictory to everything they've previously been taught about health—they seem to be oxymorons. We have been raised in a culture where we are told that bacteria is bad and should be prevented and destroyed at all cost. The truth is that fermentation is a partnership with microscopic life: enzymes and invisible friendly bacteria.

HEALTH BENEFITS OF PROBIOTIC DRINKS

"Fermentation is part health regimen, part gourmet art, part practical food preservation, part multicultural adventure, part activism, even part spiritual path as it affirms again and again the underlying interconnectedness of all."
—Sandor Elixir Katz from *Wild Fermentation*

Fermented probiotic drinks are all the craze these days. Every health-food store and natural-food shop has large beverage coolers full of colorful, effervescent bottled drinks promoting live-cultured, alkaline-rich, raw, fermented teas, waters, and juices to replenish our intestinal tracts with friendly and health-promoting bacteria. Kombucha, perhaps the most popular probiotic drink and the focus of this book, promotes high levels of B vitamins, antioxidants, and detoxifying properties. More and more people are becoming health conscious and are interested in replacing energy-zapping and health-depleting soft drinks with these fizzy, fermented, health-promoting drinks.

There is a science and art to fermentation, and we humans are in a symbiotic relationship with these single-celled organisms and cannot exist without them. Different probiotic drinks have their own unique strains of bacteria, yeast, and microbes. Thousands of different strains of helpful bacteria and yeasts positively benefit our digestive tract and immune systems. Put simply, probiotic drinks replenish the friendly bacteria in our gut biome which, in turn, promote efficient digestion and increase energy levels.

Taking probiotic supplements is one way of getting these friendly microbes into our digestive tract; however, it's up for debate in the health community as to how many of these strains of helpful microbes make it through the digestion process into our gut. Probiotic supplements most likely do not contain the variety and quantity of microbes that a home-ferment contains. Also, it's essential to transport and store probiotic supplements carefully so that the microbes don't die and are rendered ineffective. By consuming a wide variety of probiotic home-ferments such as kombucha, ginger beer, lacto-fermented sodas and teas, kefir, kvass, and cultured fruit juices, you can ensure that you are receiving a wide variety of beneficial microbes.

Louis Pasteur, who is considered the father of microbiology, spent his life studying the lifecycles of micro-organisms. His discoveries allowed us to understand the benefits of fermented foods and drinks and quite possibly boosted consumption, as well. In addition to healthy bacteria for energy and optimal digestion, probiotic drinks contain nutrients, enzymes, vitamins, minerals, and beneficial acids and yeasts not always available to us without fermenting. Depending on the type of tea, fruit, or vegetable juice we are fermenting, we receive different enzymes, vitamins, minerals, and nutrients. Fermented drinks create lactic acid, which in balance is necessary for optimal digestion. As people age, the presence of digestive enzymes declines, which makes fermented drinks particularly beneficial for older people.

Probiotic drinks create a positive and healthy environment for our digestive tract and heal the gut from damage incurred by chemical fertilizers, pesticides, pharmaceuticals, and processed foods. What seems to be agreed upon by many doctors and practitioners of allopathic and alternative medicine is that there are both therapeutic and preventative health benefits to probiotic drinks.

The US marketplace is seeing a surge in products such as supplements, nutraceuticals, and bottle refreshments with claims about the quantity and diversity of the strains of bacteria in them. The best way to get friendly bacteria in our gut biome is the way our ancestors did it and the way we will equally benefit: by consuming the largest diversity of probiotic-rich foods.

Many juice and smoothie bars and even local pubs now carry kombucha, perhaps one of the most famous of the fermented fizzy drinks, on draft. Doctors are prescribing the consumption of probiotic drinks to their patients to achieve optimal health. Book shelves have exploded with titles such as *Kombucha, Kefir and Beyond* by Alex Lewin and Rawuel Guajardo, *Delicious Probiotic Drinks* by Julia Mueller, and *Ferment for Good: Ancient Foods For The Modern Gut* by Sharon Flynn. It's in the mainstream and it's everywhere. No matter what the latest trendy diet suggests, one thing doctors of both conventional medicine and natural medicine agree on is that probiotics have positive effects on digestion, metabolism, immune system, and mental health. Fermented probiotic drinks help repopulate our intestinal tracts with healthy friendly bacteria, which is essential to wellness. Good digestion, boosted immunity, improved brain function, and better mental health are all benefits that come with consuming nonalcoholic fermented beverages.

CHAPTER 2
Getting Started

IF YOU'VE NEVER FERMENTED BEFORE, the process may seem daunting. I got started brewing kombucha by purchasing a scoby (symbiotic colony of bacteria and yeast) on the internet for $14. A test tube the size of my little finger arrived in the mail with a very small amount of liquid inside and an even smaller speck of a scoby. At the time, I was pretty sure I had been scammed. The instructions that came with tiny scoby told me that this would help me make one gallon of home-brewed kombucha. I followed the instructions, and in twenty days, I had a batch of fizzy, delicious kombucha. Start slow, take your time. Make one batch at a time. Choose the flavors of teas and fruit juices that you are most familiar with. You can always continue to experiment and try new things later. Take the recipes I have given you in this book and make your own creations. By playing around/experimenting with different fruits, vegetables, juices, herbs, spices, teas, flowers, and sugars, the possibilities are endless. As I have told students in many fermentation classes, "Your only limitation is your own creativity." The goal of this book is to give you clear, concise, and confidence-boosting information. Start with the right equipment.

SETTING YOURSELF UP FOR SUCCESS

Sanitation
Sterilization is key to ensuring your batches of fermented liquids are successful. Sanitation and sterilization ensure that you create conditions in which naturally occurring wild organisms thrive and

proliferate. Washing your equipment, especially your jars and fermentation vessels, with antibacterial dish soap is good. Nowadays, you can choose from many options in your grocery store shelves. I encourage you to use a nontoxic biodegradable dish soap made from natural ingredients. Conventional dish soaps are often made from harsh disinfectant chemicals that also contain artificial coloring agents, fragrances, and skin irritants. Our goal is to promote the growth of beneficial microbial life, and we want to minimize anything that would disrupt that, especially chemical residue. I encourage you to use the highest quality chemical-free organic ingredients, which includes the cleaning agents you use to prepare, disinfect, and sterilize your equipment. A hot dishwasher, preferably with a "sanitize" setting, will do the job for cleaning and sanitizing your kitchen equipment.

One method used specifically for sterilizing your kombucha containers is pouring boiling water in your glass jars, swishing it around, and allowing to air dry. Another option is, after thoroughly washing your jars, to place them on a metal tray and put them in your oven at 350°F for 10 minutes. Some fermentation enthusiasts swear by using only hot water and vinegar to sanitize their equipment to ensure no chemical residue is leftover that may inhibit their ferments from flourishing.

Many factors will affect the flavor, consistency (how effervescent they are), and speed at which your brews ferment. Especially with ferments like kombucha, which require a previous batch to inoculate and make sequential batches, the amount of sugar left over and the quantity of microbes in the batch will affect the outcome of the next batch brewed. Some of these factors include:

- Temperature
- Tea type
- Tea quality
- Sugar type (see Sugar section below)
- Amount of sugar used
- Amount of sugar left from the first batch (ferment)

- Maturity of the culture and the quantity of probiotics feeding on the sugar in the "starter tea."

Temperature is one of the biggest things that will affect the speed at which your kombucha ferments. The warmer the environment, the faster your kombucha will brew. In colder winter months, your kombucha may take longer. One thing I used to do when I brewed my kombucha and other ferments in Milwaukee, Wisconsin, in the winter was keep my kombucha in the oven with the oven light on. I had a small oven thermometer in there, and I was able to change the oven light bulb, bigger or smaller, to adjust the heat. Later, when I worked at a wellness center, we built an insulated fermentation cupboard.

Equipment

The following is what you should have on hand to start your fermented beverage journey!

- Scoby (Symbiotic Colony of Bacteria and Yeast)
- 1 cup of starter tea from a previous batch of mature kombucha
- Milk kefir grains (for making kefir)
- Water kefir grains (for making water kefir)
- Fine strainer (preferably non-metal)
- Sterilized glass jars
- Kitchen towels
- Cheese cloth, paper towels, or coffee filters
- Thermometer
- Large handkerchiefs
- Large rubber band
- Wooden spoon for stirring and mixing
- Juicer (optional for second ferments)

You may also want glass jugs of various sizes, glass jars, airlocks, stoppers, and lids. You don't need every single tool for every recipe. You may find that a bandana or a torn-up T-shirt work better than a piece of cheese cloth or a coffee filter. You may find that a traditional sauerkraut or kimchi crock or ceramic cookie jar works better than a large,

glass, deli-style pickle or mayonnaise jar. Some fermentation experts say that you should never use metal because it negatively interacts with the microbes and affects the quality of the fermentation, so stirring with a metal spoon and straining with a meatal strainer is forbidden. Other well-respected fermenters report that minimal use of metal is completely fine and that there is no need to go buy a wooden spoon or a plastic strainer. Modify and adapt your equipment to your own kitchen and your unique needs. The important thing to remember is that you don't need every last piece of equipment that I have listed here. If you are an aspiring minimalist, a mason jar and a tablespoon will be enough. Evaluate the tools you already have in your kitchen and see what else you may need to invest in.

When it comes to jars, mason jars are the most common and durable in the United States. They are inexpensive durable glass jars designed for canning that can withstand very high heat. They come in two common mouth sizes: standard mouth (70 millimeters) and wide mouth (86 millimeters), and they usually come with a two-part metal lid. The metal lids can begin to corrode and rust over time, especially if you wash them in the dishwasher. You can buy plastic lids that fit your jars at most grocery or home goods stores. The plastic lids are durable, easy to clean, and don't rust or deteriorate like the metal ones. There are various brand names such as Kerr, Ball, Bernardin, Jarden, Anchor Hocking, Bormioli, and Libbey. Most of the ones in my kitchen I found at thrift stores and garage sales. Mason jars are great for fermenting as well as storing your brews. Some brewers of kombucha and other ferments swear by glass jugs, growlers, wine bottles with corks, Grolsch-style bottles, and lids with airlocks. You may want to investigate these different bottles and methods for storage. I have always used large, glass deli-style pickle jars for fermenting and large quart-sized mason jars for storage. This has been more than enough for me.

When talking about lids, it's also important to discuss airlocks and managing gasses. Some ferments require breathing while

they are fermenting, which means not putting a tight lid on. This is considered *aerobic fermentation*. Other ferments you will learn about require a lid on the jar or crock. Anytime you have a tight lid, pressure builds inside. If you are fermenting in a mason jar, one option is to leave the lid on loosely, which will allow the air to slowly escape. Another option is to "burp" your ferment periodically, which involves unscrewing the lid long enough to hear the decompressing hissing sound and then screwing the lid back on tight again. You can also purchase airtight locks.

If you're doing an open ferment, make sure you still cover your brew with a cloth napkin, a handkerchief, a paper towel, or a coffee filter and securely fasten it with a rubber band or piece of twine. Animals, insects, dust, dirt, and other undesirable things that may affect the integrity of your ferment will probably get in there with the lid off.

Measurements

In the United States, we use US customary units, which are teaspoons, tablespoons, ounces, cups, pints, quarts, and gallons. Nearly the rest of the world uses the metric system, which includes grams for weight, liters for volume, milliliters, and milligrams. Depending on where you are in the world and what units of measurement you'll be using, the following chart may be helpful. For the sake of ease and consistency, I will be using US customary unites for the recipes and ingredients throughout the book. I have never needed more than measuring cups and measuring spoons (teaspoons and tablespoons) to make any of the ferments in this book. You may want to invest in a small kitchen scale, as well.

US	Metric
1 pound	0.45 Kilogram
1 quart	.95 Liter
1 ounce	28.35 grams
1 ounce	29.57 milliliters
1 tablespoon	14 grams
1 tablespoon	14.8 milliliters
1 teaspoon	4 grams
1 teaspoon	4.9 milliliters

A Note About Juicing

I am a juicing fanatic! I not only love the energizing feeling of fresh fruit and vegetable juice, but I love the taste! I have worked in juice and smoothie bars in the past, and the mixologist in me loves blending and combining flavors of local and exotic fruits, vegetables, greens, and herbs. It's understandable if someone who picked up this book is only interested in the vast and unique flavor profiles of the fermented beverages. However, many people who are intrigued with the world of fermentation are also concerned with health, longevity, and disease prevention (I legally can't say *cure*). Fresh fruit and vegetable juicing is a simple and delicious way to get vitamins, minerals, antioxidants, phytonutrients, and enzymes into our bodies. Some of the recipes involving a second ferment call for juice. "Mocktails" recipes call for adding fruit juice for additional flavor and color. I strongly encourage you to use fresh juice that you extract in your own kitchen. After all, this is a book about DIY kitchen projects that involve experimentation and self-reliance to create affordable, high-integrity recipes for health and flavor. Why not do the extra step and purchase a juicer? Juicers can be found secondhand on eBay and Craigslist and at rummage and garage sales. They can also be purchased brand-new with prices ranging from $25 to $2,000. To make the recipes in this book, you can easily get by with a modestly priced model. A juicer is a worthwhile investment in your and your family's health and will provide nourishment for years to come.

Choosing the Right Ingredients

Water

Water quality is essential. Most municipal tap water contains impurities, chlorine, and fluoride. Water impurities can be classified into one of three categories: unintentional toxic impurities, intentional toxic impurities, and trace minerals. Chlorine is an intentional impurity that exists in many cities' tap water in the United States; it's intended to inhibit the growth of bacteria/microbes. This poses a problem since it inhibits the growth of bacteria in your ferments as well as in your digestive tract. Many people in the health community swear by spring water. Other tea enthusiasts, concerned with extracting as much of the medicinal properties from the tea, swear by distilled water. The most important thing is that you use purified water free of chlorine or any other harmful chemical that would inhibit the growth of friendly bacteria in your fermented concoctions. If you do not have a spring in

your backyard or a comprehensive water filter in your home, you can buy gallon jugs of spring water or distilled water at your local grocery store.

S.C.O.B.Y

As mentioned earlier, scoby stands for Symbiotic Colony of Bacteria and Yeast. This colony transforms your sweet tea into the fizzy probiotic health tonic known as kombucha. Your scoby combined with a cup of mature kombucha starts your brew. A scoby looks like a flat, rubbery frisbee. They can be as thin as a few centimeters or as thick as a few inches. As I stated earlier, I started with a very small scoby, which turned into hundreds (maybe thousands) of gallons of kombucha for my family, friends, and me. That same fingernail-sized scoby has helped me make continuous brew for over a decade of home fermenting.

Sugar

When it comes to feed-
ing your fermentation,
sugar is key. Sugar with
the highest concentra-
tion of sweetness usu-
ally works best. Any of
the sugars listed below
can be used to brew
kombucha. People are
often concerned about
the quantity of sugar in
kombucha and always
want to use less. The
truth is that the major-

ity of the sugar is completely consumed by the fermentation. In fact,
the kombucha cannot ferment without sugar. The standard amount
of sugar for a batch of kombucha is 1 cup. Don't use any less. The
sugars listed below can also be used for any of the other fermentations in this book, except Jun, which exclusively feeds on honey.

- White granulated sugar
- Brown sugar
- Raw sugar, demerara sugar, muscovado, turbinado, or
  Sucanat
- Panela, piloncillo, or Jiggery (palm sugar)
- Molasses
- Coconut sugar
- Honey
- Maple syrup
- Aguamiel de maguey (sap from the Mexican maguey plant)

There are ongoing debates in the fermentation communities
as to what sugar is best. Most sugars will work fine, but different
"brewers" have their preferences. I encourage you to use different combinations of the aforementioned sugars. Experiment and
see what flavors you like and what your fermentations respond to.

I know some people who swear that plain white sugar makes the absolute best kombucha. I choose to stay away from white sugar for my physical and mental health, but you should do what works best for you and your grocery budget.

Artificial sweeteners such as aspartame, saccharine, xylitol, and sucralose cannot be used to brew fermented beverages. Microbes do not recognize and cannot digest these sweeteners. Natural, non-caloric sweeteners such as stevia also cannot be used in your fermentation recipes because they don't contain the food the kombucha needs: sugar. Kombucha fermentation breaks down sucrose into fructose and glucose. This feeds the yeast, which feeds the bacteria, which feeds you.

It is also suggested to avoid using raw honey because the naturally occurring bacteria in raw, unfiltered honey will fight with your colony of bacteria and yeast for dominance. Raw honey contains its own unique colony of bacteria that may adversely affect your culture.

Tea Selection

Black tea and green tea are the most optimal teas for brewing the best kombucha. I have also brewed batches with rioboos, yerba maté, hibiscus, and ginger teas. The most important thing to remember is that the scoby feeds best off compounds in black and green tea. If you use other herbal teas, I suggest you use half and half: 50% black or green tea and 50% other tea. It is also important that any tea you use has not been flavored. Many times, tea is flavored by adding a flavoring agent in the form of an oil such as orange, mint, citrus, bergamot, or clove. These oils will inhibit the growth of the friendly bacteria and may cause your batch to go bad.

Hardcore kombucha purists would lynch me for suggesting that teas other than black tea for kombucha and green tea for Jun should ever be used. Truthfully, if you want to grow and nourish the highest quality batch of kombucha that packs the probiotic punch and health benefits you're looking for, then nourishing your kombucha with black tea is going to be best. Remember what French scientist Claude Bernard said about the importance of "terrain" when it comes to nourishing our friendly gut microbes and

fighting off unfriendly pathogens and infectious microorganisms? It's the same with nourishing and caring for your kombucha. If you want the healthiest fermentation with the highest nutritional output and the best flavor, you must use the ingredients that nourish and support the kombucha properly.

Keeping Your Scoby Healthy: Making a Scoby Hotel

Once you have finished your first batch of kombucha, you'll want to keep your scoby healthy for future batches or to give to another person as a gift.

Grab a large jar similar to the one you fermented your kombucha in, or you can get a sealable 7-cup glass container. Place all of

your scobys in the glass jar and add freshly prepared sweet tea to preserve and nourish your scobys.

To prepare your sweet tea, boil 3 cups of water, remove from heat, and add 4 tea bags. Allow to steep for 10 minutes. Remove the tea bags, add ½ cup of sugar, and stir until it dissolves. Let it cool to room temperature and then add the sweet tea to your scoby hotel. This will nourish your scobys until you need to use them.

Common Kombucha Brewing Mistakes

I thought it was important to add this section because when a brewing experience goes badly, a first-time brewer can feel defeated. Perhaps they will feel that kombucha is too complicated or even dangerous and abandon all confidence of ever brewing it again. They may even stop drinking the life-giving brew altogether. This book was created to empower and educate you on making home-fermented probiotic drinks and help you fearlessly revitalize the fading art of traditional fermentation. Your health and the health of your family and community depends on it.

Common brewing mistakes to avoid making include:

1. Not using a quality scoby for a starter.
2. Not properly sterilizing or sanitizing your equipment.
3. Not using enough sugar.
4. Using a non-caloric sweetener.
5. Not using purified water and tea.
6. Not using enough starter tea. (You need 1 to 2 cups. The source should be of the same integrity as your scoby if possible.)
7. Not using strong enough starter tea.
8. Trying to start a batch from a store-bought brand that has been pasteurized, flavored, filtered, or compromised.
9. Brewing your kombucha with anything other than thoroughly cleaned and sanitized glass. No plastic, no stainless steel, or no metal.
10. Storing your scoby in the fridge and not in your scoby hotel.

CHAPTER 3
Kombucha, the Wonder Drink

"Like yogurt and cheese and many other fermented
foods, Kombucha is not the product of one specific,
fixed globally constant menagerie of microbes,
in precise ratios—it's a descriptive label fitting a category
of foods with similar characteristics."
—Alex Lewin and Raquel Guajardo,
in *Kombucha, Kefir, and Beyond*

IN THIS CHAPTER, I SHARE with you a variety of easy-to-follow recipes made from a simple batch of kombucha or Jun. Kombucha is brewed with a disaccharide and Jun is brewed with a monosaccharide (honey). Both kombucha and Jun are loaded with powerful antioxidants, enzymes, B vitamins, and glucaric acid, which is beneficial for removing toxins from the liver. Kombucha should never smell or taste bad. It should taste slightly sweet and slightly like vinegar. If it's allowed to brew too long, it will taste and smell strongly like vinegar.

Easy Kombucha Recipe

Ingredients

1 gallon distilled or purified water

8 green or black tea bags

1 cup sugar

1 cup mature kombucha ("starter tea") with scoby or "mother
mushroom"

Instructions

1. Heat the gallon of purified water in
   a large pot on the stove and add your
   green tea bags. Allow to steep for 3 to
   30 minutes depending on how strong
   you'd like your tea.

2. Remove your tea bags and stir in
   sugar until it dissolves, allowing it to
   cool to room temperature.

3. When tea is sufficiently cool, add
   your mature kombucha and scoby.
   Stir it all together to inoculate your
   batch of tea. Transfer to a gallon glass jar or fermentation
   crock and cover with a cloth.

4. Cover with a cloth and secure with a rubber band. Place in a
   warm place. It should be ready in 14 to 20 days. It will taste
   between sweet and sour. It may be fizzy. Enjoy!!

Easy Jun Recipe

The difference between Jun and kombucha is that Jun is brewed with green tea and it feeds exclusively on honey, a monosaccharide. This makes it ferment faster. Kombucha feeds on a disaccharide, which takes longer to break down. Depending on the temperature at which you keep your Jun, it can be ready anywhere between 4 days and 2 weeks. As explain earlier in this book, I once heard Jun described as the "honey-based champagne of kombucha," which is certainly an accurate way to describe this delicious fermentation.

Ingredients

1 gallon purified water

7–8 green tea bags

1 cup honey

1 Jun scoby

1 cup Jun starter tea

Instructions

1. Heat the gallon of purified water in a large pot on the stove, and add your green tea bags. Allow the tea to steep for 3 to 30 minutes depending on how strong you like your tea.

2. Remove your tea bags and allow the tea to cool before mixing in your honey. It doesn't have to cool to room temperature. Testing it with your finger is good enough. Slightly warm tea will help the honey dissolve easier.

3. When tea is sufficiently cool, add your cup of Jun tea culture and your scoby. Stir it all together with a wooden spoon to impregnate your batch of tea.

4. Cover with a cloth and secure with a rubber band. Place in a warm place with airflow that is out of direct sun.

5. In 4 to 14 days, it will be ready. It will taste between sweet and sour. The more sour it is, the less sugar is leftover. Your batch may be fizzy, but, similar to kombucha, Jun can be made even more fizzy by doing a second ferment.

A Note about Honey Quality

There are many different kinds of honey in the world. The flavor and nutritional quality can vary depending on the region the honey comes from, the type of bees that made it, and the type of flowers that the bees had access to. Wildflower honey, buckwheat honey, blueberry honey, and Manuka honey are just a few of the popular honeys sold and promoted for their unique flavor and health benefits. Honey has a different concentration of sweetener (sucrose) than the previously mentioned granulated sugars. Jun feeds on one sugar while kombucha feeds on multiple sugars.

Flavoring and Second Fermentation

There are two common ways to flavor your kombucha: one is to add juices, fruits, herbs, and spices to your already brewed batch of kombucha, mix together, and refrigerate or enjoy immediately. The other is to add fruit, sugar, and juices to an existing batch of mature kombucha and re-bottle it as a second fermentation. The benefit of a second ferment is that it makes your kombucha fizzy or effervescent and creates deep and rich flavor profiles. It is important to note that if you add store-bought pasteurized fruit juice to your kombucha for a second ferment, it will not become as fizzy and effervescent the way a second ferment does when you add real fruit or 100% fresh fruit juice.

For years, I worked as a bartender and I have always been inspired by the many unique infusions and decoctions that bartenders use in craft cocktails. The majority of the recipes that I share in this section are flavored by adding juices, extracts, and spices to mature batches of already existing kombucha. There are a lot of options for giving your kombucha flavor and fizz. Fresh fruit and both culinary and medicinal herbs are my favorite ingredients to add before second fermentation.

I typically do a second ferment on kombucha, kefir, and Jun. Once your kombucha is done fermenting, the majority of the sugar is gone. Adding fruit, juice, honey, or additional sugar is how you get the fizzy or effervescent texture.

If flavoring with fresh, frozen, or dried fruit, start with 10 to 30% fruit and 70 to 90% kombucha. If flavoring with herbs, the variety and strength of the herbs varies greatly. Experiment to come up with the best ratios and combinations to fit your taste preferences. For flavor extracts such as almond or vanilla extract, start with ¼ teaspoon extract per cup of kombucha and adjust to taste. Remember the flavor will continue to develop during the second fermentation period.

I have included many different recipes in this book, but I didn't even come close to including all the possible flavoring options or potential. Culinary and medicinal herbs, fresh and dried fruit, spices and extracts can all be used. Possible flavor combinations include blueberry vanilla, strawberry mint, mango turmeric, and beyond!

A Note about Combustion

When flavoring your kombucha with a second fermentation, there's always potential for your jars or bottles to combust. You will get the best results from your second fermentation by having truly airtight bottles. The goal is for your kombucha to become fizzy and have a new texture and flavor profile. Before bottling for your second fermentation, check your bottles for cracks or imperfections that may cause weaknesses and can lead to explosions.

The general rule is to leave your second fermentation bottled in a warm, dark place for 2 to 4 days before refrigerating. Some brewers will leave their second ferments out of the refrigerator for up to 14 days, but it is suggested that you "burp" (unscrew the lids momentarily to release pressure) your bottles daily to prevent too much pressure from building up. There is a variety of opinions on how long both initial and secondary ferments should take. Taste it daily and adjust it to your personal taste preferences. As I explained earlier, many factors will affect how fast your fermentation takes to mature: temperature, type of sugar, quantity of sugar, amount of microbes in the initial starter tea. If the bottles have been fermenting on your counter for the last few days, they may have developed quite a lot of pressure in the bottles. When you open them, they may bubble up all over the place like a shaken beer or soda. I suggest placing a towel or piece of cloth over the top of the bottle or jar and pointing it away from your face when attempting to open.

FLAVOR IDEAS AND RECIPES

I offer two methods to flavoring your kombucha. Method one allows you to make something of a kombucha cocktail where you are adding fruit juice and ingredients to a mature batch of kombucha, which you can enjoy immediately. By adding fruit juice, you slightly dilute the effervescent nature of the kombucha, but not by much. You can drink it right away; however, the longer it sits in your refrigerator, the more the flavors will slowly begin to weave themselves together.

A second ferment is like creating an entire second batch of kombucha, but where the scoby is now feeding off of the sugars from the fruit or the fruit juices. A second ferment is fizzier and has a different and increased nutrition profile. Method one is great for creating different day to day kombucha flavors, especially when you may be entertaining guests and you want to offer multiple delicious alternatives to alcoholic drinks or sodas.

Cranberry Hibiscus Kombucha

Hibiscus and cranberry go brilliantly together due to their similar flavor profiles. Hibiscus is a medicinal tisane high in vitamin C and consumed in tea form to lower blood pressure and support healthy liver function. It has fruity, sweet, sour, and astringent notes. Cranberries are a very nutritious berry native to North America that contain powerful antioxidants. Cranberries are low in sugar and classically described as fruity, tart, and slightly bitter. Brewing a batch of kombucha with hibiscus and combining it with the zesty tartness of cranberries creates a nutritious, refreshing, and energizing probiotic drink.

First Ferment

Ingredients

1 gallon purified for distilled water
4 black tea bags
4 hibiscus tea bags
1 cup sugar
1 cup living kombucha with scoby or "mother mushroom"
1 cup unsweetened cranberry juice

Instructions

1. Make a gallon batch of kombucha with half black tea, half hibiscus tea bag, sugar, and scoby (see page 39 to easy instructions).
2. Add 1 cup of unsweetened organic cranberry juice to 1 gallon of mature kombucha.
3. Enjoy immediately or store in refrigerator. As it sits in the refrigerator, the flavors will continue to blend together and become stronger and more full flavored.

Second Ferment

Ingredients

¾ gallon Hibiscus Kombucha
1 cup sugar
1 cup fresh cranberry juice or 2 cups fresh cranberries individually halved or mashed

Instructions

1. Combine the Hibiscus Kombucha with the sugar and cranberry juice or fresh cranberries.
2. Mix until all the sugar is dissolved.
3. Divide the contents among 4 sealable quart-sized mason jars and tightly secure the lids.
4. Set on your kitchen counter for 3 to 4 days.
5. Point away from your face and open slowly. It should taste tart and fruity.

Cranberry and hibiscus have deliciously tart complementary flavors. This brew can be poured over ice and enjoyed as a cocktail alternative or as a thirst-quenching summer refreshment. Add lemon and/or mint. Enjoy!

Goji Ginger Cayenne Kombucha

Goji berries, also known as Wolfberries, are reddish orange and are considered one of the world's most nutrient-dense superfoods. The have a sour, earthy flavor that mildly resembles a tomato. You can read more about them in chapter 8: Superfoods.

First Ferment

Ingredients

I gallon purified or distilled water

4 black tea bags

8 inches fresh ginger root

I cup sugar

I cup living kombucha with scoby or "mother mushroom"

½ cup fresh-squeezed lemon juice

½ cup dried goji berries

I½ teaspoons cayenne pepper

Instructions

1. Brew a batch of kombucha with 4 black tea bags and approximately 8 inches of ginger sliced into small pieces (plus sugar, plus scoby) using the directions on page 39. The ginger combined with the black tea will give this brew a slightly spicy and tingly texture and flavor similar to ginger beer. You can brew the batch of kombucha with only ginger, but you'll deprive the scoby of its essential foods source. The combination of the two ensures that you are feeding the scoby properly with the black tea while infusing the batch with the flavor and medicinal properties of ginger. Just as you would remove your tea bags, you will also strain out the ginger.

2. When your brew is ready, add ½ cup lemon juice, ½ cup goji berries, and 1½ teaspoons cayenne pepper.

3. Mix the ingredients together, pour into smaller jars, and evenly distribute the goji berries, allowing them to float around and pleasantly flavor the batch.

Method 2: Second Ferment

Ingredients

1 gallon half-ginger half-black tea kombucha (see page 48)
½ cup fresh-squeezed lemon juice
½ cup dried goji berries
1½ teaspoons cayenne pepper
1 cup sugar

Instructions

1. Brew a 1-gallon batch of ginger black tea kombucha as was explained in the first step of the previous recipe.

2. Add the goji berries, cayenne pepper, lemon juice, and sugar. Mix until the sugar disolves.

3. Pour the contents into 8-quart jars with scalable jars and secure the lids tightly.

4. Set the jars in a warm, dark place and allow to ferment for 3 to 4 days. When the second fermentation is complete, you can keep the goji berries in your kombucha or strain them out. Point away from your face and slowly unscrew the lids when you are ready to enjoy.

Pineapple Basil Kombucha

This drink includes a subtle herbal sweetness from the basil that goes astoundingly well with the sweet tartness of pineapple. I love basil, and when I make this recipe, I don't measure exactly (and I probably throw in far more basil than the average person). The measurements in this recipe are to give you a basic idea for what creates a balanced flavor. When it's summer and Italian basil is growing like crazy, you can find it cheap and abundant at local farmers' markets. In addition to tasting wonderful, basil has anti-inflammatory properties, it's immune boosting, mood elevating, and was celebrated in Italy, not just as a culinary herb, but also medicinally as an aphrodisiac. As I discussed earlier in the section on second fermentations, the strength of herbs varies greatly. Experiment with the strength and intensity that works best for your palate.

First Ferment

Ingredients
1 gallon mature homemade kombucha (see page 39)
3 cups fresh pineapple
2 cups fresh basil

Instructions
1. Take 1 gallon of mature homemade kombucha.
2. Put through your juicer 3 cups of fresh pineapple (about ¾ of an average pineapple) and 2 cups of fresh basil.
3. Add the fresh pineapple basil juice to the kombucha and mix well.
4. You can drink it instantly or bottle it and enjoy the next day. The longer it sits, the more the kombucha will feed on the sugars in the pineapple juice and the flavors will combine.

Second Ferment continued on page 52

Second Ferment

Ingredients

1 gallon homemade mature kombucha (page 39)
2 cups fresh pineapple juice
1 cup fresh basil
4 teaspoons sugar

Instructions

1. Take 1 gallon of a batch of homemade mature kombucha.
2. Add fresh pineapple juice.
3. Chop up 1 cup of fresh basil. This can be done on a cutting board using a knife or in a mortar and pestle. Another option is to place the basil in a food processor and pulse it a few times. The goal is to break down the basil so that the flavors infuse your kombucha during the second ferment. You can substitute dried basil for fresh, but you will never get the full flavor. When using dried basil, use half the amount that a recipe calls for. In the case of this recipe, you would use ½ cup dried basil.
4. Stir the pineapple juice and basil together, allowing the flavors to mix and impregnate the batch.
5. Pour the mixture into 16-ounce sealable jars and fill up three-quarters of the way and add ½ teaspoon of sugar to each jar (8 jars). Seal the jars tight and allow to sit in a warm dark place for 3 to 4 days.
6. When ready to drink, point the bottles away from your face and carefully open.
7. Some people prefer to use a small hole strainer to strain the kombucha into a glass and discard the leaves and pulp. You also have the option of eating the fruit and leaves leftover from the second ferment if you don't want to miss out on a single bit of nutrition and fiber.
8. Sip and enjoy!

Coffee Kombucha

Yes, you read this correctly: you *can* brew coffee kombucha. Coffee is a controversial beverage in the realm of nutritional health, but it has deep cultural and historical significance and, for the sake of this book, I found it necessary to include this recipe. People have a very emotional connection to coffee. Many people LOVE IT! It turns out that you can easily ferment a batch of kombucha by using coffee as a liquid base. In addition to using non-chlorinated purified water, I also encourage you to use organic coffee. You want to be using the highest-quality ingredients to minimize chemical exposure, which would compromise the growth of your scoby. Full disclosure: Coffee Kombucha is a taste bud–popping acquired taste.

Use an extra scoby that you intend on throwing away after use since you won't want to use it to make another batch. Coffee is already naturally very acidic, which allows the batch to brew faster. I add the black tea bags to ensure the scoby gets fed properly even though, in all actuality, this is not a recipe for creating the highest-quality, most nutrient-dense kombucha. It's more of a fun kitchen experiment for the sake of getting a healthy probiotic drink in your body using creative means. I suggest doing a second ferment for the sake of the flavor. After the first ferment, it's quite bitter.

First Ferment

Ingredients

1¼ cups organic coffee grounds
1 gallon purified water
4 black tea bags
1 cup sugar
1 cup mature kombucha ("starter tea")
1 scoby

Instructions

1. Heat your water until *just before* boiling and add ¾ cup of ground coffee and 4 black tea bags. Stir.

Continued on page 54

2. Allow the coffee and tea to steep for 3 to 5 minutes before pouring through cheese cloth or a small-hole strainer. The longer you steep your coffee, the stronger the flavor.

3. While the coffee and tea mixture is still hot, pour it in to your jar or fermentation receptacle, add your sugar, and mix well until it dissolves.

4. When the coffee cools to room temperature, stir in 1 cup of mature kombucha and your scoby.

5. Secure a cloth over the top with twine or a rubber band and place in a warm, dark place. As stated earlier, coffee kombucha can sometimes mature much faster due to its acidic nature.

6. Allow your coffee kombucha to ferment for 5 to 14 days. Test it periodically, and enjoy it when it has matured enough to meet your taste preferences.

Second Ferment

Ingredients

16 ounces Coffee Kombucha
½ cup sugar

Instructions

1. Brew 16 ounces of coffee kombucha, or use the brew from from first fermentation.

2. Add sugar and mix until dissolved.

3. Pour contents into quart-sized jars and seal lids tightly.

4. Allow to ferment for 3 to 4 days in a warm, dark place. When ready, point away from your face and unscrew the lids slowly. Enjoy!

Chai Pear Jun

Chai tea is a rich and delicious drink native to India. The traditional ingredients are a blend of black tea mixed with strong spices, like cinnamon, cardamom, nutmeg, clove, ginger, and black peppercorns. In this recipe, we focus on the black tea, ginger, cardamom, nutmeg, and cinnamon. These spices combined with honey and the juicy crisp sweetness of the pear create a uniquely delicious ferment.

First Ferment

Ingredients

3 tablespoons honey

½ cup hot water

2 cups chopped pears

1 gallon homemade mature Jun (see page 40)

2 teaspoons ground cinnamon

1 teaspoon ground ginger

½ teaspoon ground cardamom

½ teaspoon ground nutmeg

Instructions

1. Combine the honey and the hot water and stir together until it dissolves.
2. Combine the honey-water, chopped pears, mature homemade Jun, cinnamon, ginger, cardamom, and nutmeg in a one-gallon jar and stir the contents together, mixing it well.
3. Pour the contents evenly between 4 sealable quart-sized jars and tighten the lids.
4. Allow to sit out at room temperature for 2 to 3 days.
5. Point away from your face and slowly open. You can pour the contents through a cheese cloth or fine mesh if you don't want any granules from the spices in your drink. I think the whole spices add to the rustic charm of this fermentation. The finished product should be stored in the refrigerator. Sip and enjoy!

Strawberry Lime Basil Jun

I love the flavor combination of basil, strawberry, and lime. They go well in fresh juices, salads, and yes, fermentations. Make sure to use fresh lime juice since bottled lime juice has an unpleasant and stale reconstituted flavor that will negatively affect the flavor of your brew. If you find it a little too tart, you can scale back on the lime juice.

Ingredients

½ cup hot water

2 tablespoons honey

2 cups fresh strawberries, chopped (frozen will work if need be; thaw first, then chop)

1 cup fresh basil leaves, chopped

½ fresh-squeezed lime juice

¾ gallon mature homemade Jun (see page 40)

Instructions

1. Combine the honey and the hot water and stir together until it dissolves.

2. Combine the chopped strawberries, basil, lime juice, honey-water, and ¾ gallon of mature homemade Jun in a one-gallon jar, and stir the contents together, mixing it well.

3. Pour the contents evenly between 4 sealable quart-sized jars and tighten the lids.

4. Allow to sit out at room temperature for 2 to 3 days.

5. Point away from your face and slowly open. You can pour the contents through a cheese cloth or fine mesh if you don't want any strawberries or basil in your drink or enjoy as is. Sip with abandon!

Blackberry Apple Sage Jun

In this recipe we combined complementary fruits and herbs of the fall harvest. Blackberries have a sweet and slightly tart flavor that combine well with the warming and mystical earthiness of sage. When these flavors blend with the sweetness of crisp autumn apples you get a desert-like fizzy brew reminiscent of a dessert enjoyed on a brisk fall day. For this recipe the sweeter varieties of apples work the best. I would suggest Fuji, Ambrosia, Gala, Golden Delicious, or Red Delicious apples.

First Ferment

Ingredients

2 tablespoons honey

½ cup hot water

2 cups fresh blackberries

1 cup chopped fresh apples

½ cup chopped fresh sage

¾ gallon mature homemade Jun (see page 40)

Instructions

1. Combine the honey and the hot water and stir together until it dissolves.

2. Combine the blackberries, apples, sage, honey-water, and mature homemade Jun in a one-gallon jar and stir the contents together, mixing well.

3. Pour the contents evenly between 4 sealable quart-sized jars and tighten the lids.

4. Allow to sit out at room temperature for 2 to 3 days.

5. Point away from your face and slowly open. You can pour the contents through a cheese cloth or fine mesh if you don't want any blackberry seeds, leftover fruit, or pieces of sage in your drink. I like to drink it as is. Store the contents in the refrigerator. Enjoy cold, at room temperature, or over ice.

Lavender Jun with Lemon

This is a fragrant, refreshing, and visually appealing drink. The brightness in the fresh lemon brings out the floral notes and balsamic undertones of the lavender. This ferment is a fizzy and probiotic adaptation to the popular summer Lavender Lemonade, which is popular at picnics and celebratory gatherings.

Ingredients

4 cups purified water

1 cup dried lavender flowers

½ cup honey

½ cup fresh-squeezed lemon juice

¾ gallon mature homemade Jun (see page 40)

Instructions

1. Heat 4 cups of water until just before boiling.

2. Add the dried lavender flowers, and allow to steep for 5 to 10 minutes.

3. Stir in the honey while the tea is still warm and allow to cool to room temperature.

4. Combine the sweetened lavender tea (flowers still included, as they continue to flavor the fermentation), lemon juice, and ¾ gallon of mature homemade Jun in a one-gallon jar and stir the contents together, mixing well.

5. Pour the contents evenly between 4 sealable quart-sized jars and tighten the lids.

6. Allow to sit out at room temperature for 2 to 3 days.

7. Point away from your face and slowly open. You can pour the contents through a cheese cloth or fine mesh if you don't want any lavender flowers in your drink or enjoy as-is. Store the contents in the refrigerator. Enjoy cold or at room temperature. Lavender Jun with lemon is particularly refreshing over ice, similar to a summer glass of lemonade.

Citrus Bomb Kombucha Mocktail

The majority of the nutritional value in citrus fruits comes from the peel. When steeped as a tea or an infusion, fruit peels can make a ferment very flavorful but slightly bitter. In this brew, I briefly squeeze each of the pieces of citrus fruits before putting them in the jar.

Ingredients

½ lemon, sliced

I orange, sliced

¼ grapefruit, sliced

½ lime, sliced

I quart homemade mature kombucha (see page 39)

½ teaspoon sugar

Instructions

1. In a sealable, quart-sized mason jar, place all sliced citrus fruits.
2. Cover the fruit with kombucha and add sugar.
3. Seal the lid tight, and allow to sit out at room temperature for 3 to 4 days.
4. Point away from your face and slowly open.
5. Strain out the contents and enjoy!

Mint "Mojito" Kombucha

A classic mojito is a refreshing cocktail from the enchanting and forbidden Caribbean island of Cuba. It is traditionally made from combining white rum, sugar, and mint. The freshness of the mint combines beautifully with the tanginess of the lime to create a truly vibrant and refreshing drink. In this recipe we make a nonalcoholic version, which consist primarily of mature kombucha for a healthy probiotic punch.

Ingredients

4 lime wedges

6–8 fresh mint

2 teaspoons sugar

ice

¾ cup mature homemade kombucha (page 39)

½ cup carbonated mineral water

First Fermentation

Instructions

1. In a sturdy pint glass, place your lime, fresh mint, and sugar.
2. With a muddler or a wooden spoon, muddle the ingredients in the bottom of the glass until mashed and blended together.
3. Add ice, kombucha, and carbonated mineral water.
4. With a spoon or a utensil, stir the ingredients together until well mixed. If you have access to a martini shaker, you can blend the ingredients like a proper mojito, but remember that kombucha will fizz up on you and might end up all over the place.

Second Fermentation

Ingredients

16 ounces homemade mature kombucha (see page 39)
¼ cup fresh mint
4 lime wedges
½ teaspoon sugar

Instructions

1. Put the mature batch of homemade kombucha in a sealable quart jar.
2. Chop the mint by hand or place in a blender and pulse a few times. Add the chopped mint to the kombucha.
3. By hand, squeeze the lime wedges into the mint Kombucha mixture.
4. Add sugar and stir well.
5. Seal the jar and place in a warm, dark place for 2 to 4 days.
6. Point away from your face and slowly open. Strain out the mint or enjoy as is. Store the contents in the refrigerator. This concoction is best served cold or over ice.

Blackberry Kombucha "Mojito"

Many different fruits can be added to a mojito to complement the herbaceous freshness of the mint and the acidic sour of the limes. Berries go particularly well. A blackberry mojito, also referred to as a "Midnight Mojito," is crafted similar to the classic mojito, but muddled blackberries are added in addition. The inky tartness of the blackberries bring out the zesty and refreshing flavors of the mint and limes. Enjoy this beverage on a summer day!

Ingredients

4 lime wedges

¼ cup fresh mint

2 teaspoons sugar

ice

¾ cup mature homemade kombucha (see page 39)

¼ cup fresh blackberries

½ cup carbonated mineral water

First Ferment

Instructions

1. In the bottom of a pint glass or mason jar, muddle limes, mint, and sugar together.
2. Fill the glass with ice and add the kombucha.
3. Stir the ingredients together, being aware that the contents may get fizzy. (In a traditional mojito, you would shake the contents with a martini shaker. I've learned that shaking even mildly fizzy kombucha can make it go everywhere. With this recipe, I encourage you to stir the ingredients together.)
4. Garnish with mint and limes. Sip, share, and enjoy!

Second Ferment

Ingredients

16 ounces homemade mature kombucha (see page 39)
¼ cup fresh blackberries
¼ cup fresh mint
4 lime wedges
½ teaspoon sugar

Instructions

1. Put the mature batch of homemade kombucha in a quart jar.
2. Chop the mint by hand or place in a blender and pulse a few times. Add the chopped mint to the kombucha.
3. Place the blackberries in a blender or food processor and blend. Add the blended blackberries to the homemade kombucha.
4. By hand, squeeze the lime wedges into the mint-blackberry-kombucha mixture.
5. Add sugar to the mixture and stir the ingredients together.
6. Seal the jar and leave in a warm, dark place for 2 to 4 days.
7. Point away from your face and slowly open. Strain out the mint and blackberries or enjoy as is. Store the contents in the refrigerator. This recipe is best served cold or over ice.

Berry Explosion Kombucha

For this recipe, a combination of strawberries, blueberries, raspberries, and blackberries is excellent. Fresh and organic is always
better, but I have had success making this recipe by using non-
organic frozen berries, as well. Red or purple grapes, currants,
black raspberries, and cranberries could also be mixed in. Note
that this recipe will require a second fermentation and cannot be
consumed right away.

Ingredients

2 cups of fresh berries
1 gallon homemade mature kombucha (see page 39)
4 teaspoons sugar for second fermentation

Instructions

1. Place the berries in a blender, add 1 cup kombucha, and blend
    or pulse.
2. Add the berry-kombucha blend to the gallon of kombucha,
    and mix well.
3. Pour the berry-kombucha contents into 16-ounce sealable jars
    or bottles, leave three-quarters of the way full.
4. Add ½ teaspoon of sugar to each jar and seal them tightly for
    their second fermentation.
5. Leave the bottles in a warm, dark place for 2 to 4 days.
6. When ready to open, point away from your face and open
    slowly.

Grapefruit Jalapeño Kombucha

The result is a bright and refreshing probiotic drink with a mild spicy heat. It is important to note with this recipe that, unlike many of the other recipes, **this one is exclusively a second fermentation**. After all of the ingredients have been combined, they must be sealed in jars and fermented for 3 to 4 days before they can be strained and enjoyed.

Ingredients

2 cups grapefruit juice, preferably fresh
½ cup finely chopped fresh jalapeño peppers
1 gallon mature homemade kombucha (see page 39)
4 teaspoons sugar

Instructions

1. Add the grapefruit juice and then the jalapeño peppers to your kombucha. Mix the contents thoroughly.
2. Create a second fermentation by pouring the jalapeño-grapefruit mixture into 16-ounce sealable jars, filling them three quarters of the way.
3. Add ½ teaspoon sugar to each jar and seal tightly.
4. Set the jars in a warm, dark place for 2 to 4 days.
5. When ready, point away from your face and slowly open. Strain the contents through a small-hole strainer or enjoy as is.

Kombucha Sangria

This is a healthy, alcohol-free rendition of a Spanish favorite. This is a great recipe when entertaining guests who are health-conscious and would like to enjoy something celebratory and reminiscent of a cocktail. I encourage you to make the orange juice and the pineapple juice fresh. Okay, okay, since it's lacking red wine and brandy, it's nothing like true Spanish sangria, but it does create a very delicious and thirst-quenching juice cocktail great for entertaining.

Ingredients

2 cups homemade kombucha

1 cup orange juice

1 cup pineapple juice

½ cup red grapes, halved

½ cup green grapes, halved

½ cup strawberries, halved

4 slices orange

4 slices lemon

4 slices lime

Instructions

1. In a large pitcher, combine the kombucha, orange juice, and pineapple juice.
2. Add the grapes, strawberries, oranges, lemons, and limes.
3. Stir the contents together.
4. Fill two pint glasses with ice, and pour the contents over it, ensuring a generous amount of fruit gets into each glass. Garnish with a slice of lemon, lime, and orange, on the rim of the glass.
5. Other fruit options that go well with this recipe are blueberries, raspberries, peaches, apples, pears, pineapple chunks, and slices of mango.

CHAPTER 4
Kefir

IN THIS CHAPTER, I DISCUSS the origins and health benefits of the popular probiotic drink kefir. Even though it is traditionally made from cow's milk, a healthy non-dairy alternative can be made from coconut milk, making this elixir vegetarian and vegan friendly. Both dairy kefir and coconut kefir have a naturally pleasant flavor, which make them very versatile in a variety of recipes. I have included recipes for both food and drinks to show the variety of delicious and health-promoting combinations that can be created and enjoyed in your kitchen. Due to how similar kefir can be to popular foods such as yogurt, sour cream, and ice cream, it blends wonderfully with nearly all varieties of fruits. I strongly encourage anyone to fearlessly experiment in their kitchen with this fermentation technique.

Milk Kefir

Milk kefir is a probiotic fermented dairy beverage traditionally made from cow's milk. It has a sour and tangy taste similar to yogurt and a thick and creamy texture similar to a blended fruit smoothie. In fact, dairy kefir goes very well with blended fruit, and I have included different smoothie recipes that can be made with either milk kefir or its vegan-friendly alternative, coconut milk kefir.

In my research, I have found reports that kefir originated in the Central Asian Caucasus Mountains. Other accounts state that kefir comes from the Balkans, where ancient shepherds fermented kefir inside pouches made of goat leather. Some stories say that it is Russian, and folklore confirms this with a great story of conspiracy, deception, and cultural thievery. One of the most engaging accounts comes from the book *Wild Fermentation: The Flavor, Nutrition and Craft of Live Cultured Foods* by Sandor Elix Katz. According to Katz, in the early twentieth century, the "All-Russian Physicians' Society" became intrigued by the health properties of kefir and wanted to get their hands on it. The keepers of the kefir grains refused to share their coveted health secret, which forced the physicians' society to come up with a deceptive plan involving a charming female temptress. The beautiful young woman was sent to a Caucasian Prince, Bek-Mirza Barchorov, to try and obtain the kefir grains. The plan didn't work, and the young woman was kidnapped instead. To make reparations, and by order of the courts, the prince was required to let the young woman go and give her some of the cherished kefir grains. This is how the first kefir grains made it to Moscow, and to this day, kefir remains a very popular drink in Russia.

Milk kefir requires a starter similar to sourdough bread. Kefir grains, the kefir starter, are small rubbery bead-like cell structures comprising the bacteria and yeast that ferment the kefir. Kefir grains are the equivalent of the scoby used to make kombucha. Kefir is one of the simplest ferments. The healthy bacteria and yeast in the kefir grains will ferment the milk. The magic of kefir grains is that they also prevent the milk from spoiling while transforming it into a healthy probiotic beverage. The consistency is similar to buttermilk or thin, pourable yogurt. Strain out your kefir grains and use them to make your next batch. It's important to note that kefir grains are not actual grains. So, they are gluten-free. In order to keep your kefir grains healthy, it's best to keep making continuous batches of kefir. Your kefir grains will multiply, in which case you can throw the additional ones away or give them to a friend to make their own kefir. Similar to kombucha scoby, kefir grains, if kept healthy, will continue making future batches. Milk kefir grains work best with whole-fat animal milk: cows, goats, and sheep. You can make kefir with 2% and reduced fat milk, but it will take longer than with whole-fat milk. It is best to store your kefir grains in a glass of whole milk in between ferments to refresh them and liven them back up.

A Note about Dairy

Dairy gets a bad rap in the health and nutrition world. The truth is that dairy products aren't necessary for our health or survival, and many people have strong, allergic reactions to them. The idea of humans consuming something that is secreted from the mammary glands of an animal, like a cow, is strange in and of itself. The human species has only been consuming dairy products for a short period of our evolutionary history. Homo-sapiens survived without dairy products for a long time and could continue to do so. No one will suffer from or die from "dairy product deficiency." As I discussed in the introduction of this book, we humans don't only eat for health. We also eat for pleasure, sharing, comradery, celebration, and enjoyment. Dairy is one of the most popular food categories all over the world and it has deep cultural and heritage ties.

Many recipes you will find on the internet and in fermentation books call for raw, unpasteurized milk if it can be found. Raw milk is celebrated for its uncompromised protein, minerals, vitamins, and living bacteria. For fermentation enthusiasts, the living bacteria is one of the most exciting things about it. **A word of caution about raw unpasteurized milk:** People have been consuming raw, unpasteurized milk for thousands of years. In the Hindu religion, for example, milk is considered sacred and Hindus have been consuming it in its raw form for more than four thousand years. In the United States, raw milk is illegal because it has the potential for carrying dangerous bacteria such as *Salmonella, E. coli, Listeria, Campylobacter*, and other foodborne illnesses. If you are pregnant, immunocompromised, or have young children, do your research and weigh the risks with the benefits and always consult your physician. Most studies show that the risk of developing a serious illness from drinking unpasteurized milk is very low, but the risk is still there, and it's important to be informed. Some members of the fermentation community report that the beneficial cultures in the kefir will dominate in the fermentation process so much that the harmful pathogens won't be able to take hold. Regardless, be careful of where your raw milk comes from and recognize that there is a risk. Fermentation reduces, but does not completely eliminate, the risk.

Milk kefir grains can be purchased at some health-food stores or online. I have been impressed by the number of fermentation potluck groups, meet-ups, or online chat forums and communities where people are happy and willing to give kefir grains for free to anyone with the enthusiasm to play in their kitchens and make their own home-fermented kefir. See the resources section at the end of this chapter.

Similar to kombucha, the temperature of your kitchen will affect how fast your kefir is ready. Generally, when I have made both dairy and non-dairy kefirs, they have been ready in 24 hours at room temperature that was between 72°F and 84°F. The longer your kefir sits and ferments, the longer the friendly bacteria will feed on the lactose in the milk. It will continue to get more sour and fizzier. If your kefir is allowed to ferment too long, it will separate into curds and whey, look cloudy and chunky, and taste quite sour. This new consistency is still drinkable, but it will taste quite sour and unpleasant to many people. This curd-and-whey substance can still be used for making cooking projects such as dips, spreads, and salad dressings. Your kefir grains are still good and can be used again to make future batches.

Non-dairy and Vegan Friendly Alternatives

If you are someone who avoids milk due to digestive issues, it is important to note that the fermenting process changes some of the protein structures in the milk, making it easier to digest. Some people who can't tolerate milk are able to drink milk kefirs. For whatever the reason you prefer to not consume cow's milk, there are many other dairy alternatives for making kefir. Coconut, hemp, soy, almond, pumpkin (pepita) seed milk, and any other milk-like substance that comes from a nut, seed, or legume that contains proper amounts of fat can be used.

In this book, I will show you how to make coconut milk kefir because its flavor, fat content, and consistency are perfect for making a bubbly, sour, tangy, and delicious non-dairy kefir. It's created the same way that milk kefir is made but using coconut milk with your kefir grains instead.

Non-dairy milks such as coconut and almond milks won't nourish your kefir grains as well as cow's milk will. With every batch of non-dairy kefir made from the same starter, the grains will become smaller and less vibrant. Give your kefir grains a rest every second or third batch by placing them in a glass of whole milk and letting them grow again.

Milk Kefir Recipe

Here is the simple and easy-to-follow recipe of tangy, sour, and delicious kefir made specifically from cow's milk. As stated earlier, it will work best with whole milk and will be ready in 24 to 48 hours. If stored properly in the refrigerator your kefir grains will continue to make batches of creamy and delicious milk kefir. It can be enjoyed as is or used in smoothies and other recipes in place of yogurt.

Method 1: Making Kefir using Kefir Grains

Equipment

1 quart-sized mason jar
Plastic strainer
Piece of cloth, paper towel, or coffee filter
Rubber band or piece of twine

Ingredients

2 tablespoons dairy kefir grains
16 ounces whole milk

Instructions

1. Put the 2 tablespoons of kefir in the quart jar and combine with the 16 ounces of whole milk.
2. Stir the contents together.
3. Place the piece of cloth over the jar and adhere with a rubber band or piece of twine.
4. Allow to sit in a warm, undisturbed place for 24 to 48 hours.
5. When ready, strain with a fine strainer, bottle, and refrigerate the liquid.
6. Save your strained kefir grains and use them to make a new batch.

Method 2: Making Kefir Using Freeze-Dried Kefir Starter

Equipment

1 quart-sized mason jar
Plastic strainer
Piece of cloth, paper towel, or coffee filter
Rubber band or piece of twine

Ingredients

16 ounces whole milk
5 grams of freeze-dried kefir starter (1 packet)

Instructions

1. Pour 16 ounces of whole milk into a quart-sized mason jar.
2. If using refrigerated milk, heat to 70°F to 75°F.
3. Add 1 packet of starter culture and stir gently until the culture is fully dissolved.
4. Place the piece of cloth over the jar and adhere with a rubber band or piece of twine.
5. Allow to sit in a warm, undisturbed place for 24 to 48 hours.
6. When ready, it will have the consistency of heavy cream and it will smell and taste sour like Greek yogurt. No need to strain.
7. Cover the finished product with a tight lid and store in the refrigerator.

Reculturing your Kefir

Kefir made from kefir starter can be re cultured anywhere from 2 to 7 times. The exact number of batches that you can re-culture depends on the freshness of the batch and how hygienically everything is executed. It is important to re-culture within 7 days of making your last batch. Longer periods between batches may not result in successful batches.

Ingredients

16 ounces milk
¼ cup mature kefir (see page 83)

Instructions

1. Pour milk into a quart-sized mason jar.
2. If using refrigerated milk, heat to 70°F to 75°F.
3. Add mature kefir from the previous batch and stir gently.
4. Cover the container with cloth and secure with a rubber band.
5. Place in a warm, undisturbed spot for 12 to 16 hours.
6. Cover the finished product with a tight lid and store in the refrigerator.

Coconut Milk

The source of your coconut milk is important when it comes to crafting good-quality coconut milk kefir. You can use homemade coconut milk (my preference), or you can use store-bought canned variety. If using store-bought coconut milk, read labels and avoid brands that use additives and sweeteners. Additives and sweeteners can be hard on the kefir grains and can affect the outcome of your batch. Guar gum is a typical stabilizing agent in canned coconut milk and doesn't seem to be a problem. I have included two different recipes on how to make coconut milk. The first one involves using young coconuts, which contain a silkier, more gelatinous coconut meat and a sweeter water inside, which when blended, together create a thicker and creamier milk that resembles "coconut cream." With this recipe you will be able to create a kefir that is similar to coconut yogurt.

The second recipe uses mature coconuts, which contain a firmer, nuttier meat that requires grinding or grating. The water inside is usually sour and void of flavor and nutrition and can be discarded. This second method allows you to make a blended milk that is similar to the texture and viscosity of cow's milk. Both methods work for fermenting quality kefir. In some areas of the world, coconuts are incredibly abundant and they may even grow in your yard. In other parts of the world they may cost you $5 a piece in the grocery store. Where I am from in Milwaukee, Wisconsin, mature coconuts cost around $2 a piece and young coconuts cost between $3 and $4 a piece. This may affect your choice of ingredients depending on where you live and what you have access to. If you find that coconuts are quite expensive where you live, think of it as an investment in your health.

Method 1:

Equipment
high-powered blender
large knife or meat cleaver
sturdy metal spoon

Ingredients
1 young coconut
1–2 cups additional coconut water or plain purified water

Instructions
1. Take your large kitchen knife or meat clever and crack open the top of your young coconut. There are many tutorial videos on the internet to show you how to do this. Be careful and watch your fingers!
2. Pour the water from the young coconut into your high-powered blender. Young coconuts can contain anywhere from 12 to 20 ounces of water depending on the type of coconut and their maturity level.
3. Once the coconut has been emptied of its liquid, split your coconut open wider using your kitchen knife.

Continued on page 88

4. Use your spoon to scrape the young coconut meat from the opened coconut and put it in the blender.

5. Blend the coconut meat and coconut water for 20 seconds or until thick and creamy. Depending on the coconut meat-to-water ratio, you may want to add additional water to the blended coconut milk. The thicker your coconut milk, the thicker your kefir will become when it ferments. I think homemade, thick-blended coconut milk makes the best tasting kefir.

Method 2:

Equipment

stove
high-powered blender
food processor or cheese grater
nut milk bag, cheese cloth, butter muslin, or fine strainer
large kitchen knife or meat clever
butter knife

Ingredients

1 large mature coconut
4 cups purified water
½ teaspoon guar gum (optional)

Instructions

1. Hold your mature coconut over the sink or a large bowl and strike it with the back of the knife. It may not crack open in one blow, so you may need to turn the coconut a quarter turn and strike it again. Continue turning the coconut and striking it with the back of the knife until it breaks open.

2. The coconut will have a layer of 1 to 1½ inch–thick dense meat on the inside. Don't worry about saving the water. Mature coconut water is not as nutritious or flavorful as young coconut water.

3. Take your butter knife and wedge it between the coconut meat and the coconut shell. Turn frequently and pry the meat away

from the shell. This may take a while since the coconut meat can adhere to the inside of the shell. It is important to use a sturdy, dull knife like a butter knife since the tip of sharp kitchen knives are quite fragile and can easily break off when trying to remove coconut meat from the shell.

4. Make your shredded coconut by using a cheese grater or a food processor fitted with a shredding disk or grating disk. Set aside 2 cups of shredded coconut.

5. Put the water in a sauce pan and heat it on the stove. Make it hot, as if you were to brew tea, but don't bring it to a boil.

6. Add the freshly shredded coconut to the hot water.

7. Let the coconut steep like tea for about 10 minutes.

8. Place the water and coconut in your blender and blend on high for about 20 seconds.

9. Pour the blended contents through your nut milk bag, butter muslin, or fine strainer over a bowl.

10. Use your hands to squeeze the coconut to wring out as much liquid as possible.

11. Pour the homemade coconut milk into a jar or pitcher, mix in your guar gum, and refrigerate. It will keep in the refrigerator up for five days. Use this to make your coconut milk kefir.

Note: You can also make this recipe using store-bought shredded coconut. You want to make sure that it is unsweetened and doesn't contain any coloring or preservatives. You'll need 2 cups unsweetened shredded coconut.

Coconut Milk Kefir

Coconut milk kefir is a rich non-dairy alternative to traditional cow's milk based kefir. Coconut has a viscous, sweet, and nutty flavor that makes this fermentation a popular favorite. In addition to being absolutely delicious, coconut is one of the worlds superfoods, containing a high concentration of nutrients and beneficial fats that nourish the human body.

Equipment

1 quart-sized mason jar
plastic strainer
piece of cloth, paper towel, or coffee filter
rubber band or piece of twine

Ingredients

16 ounces coconut milk

2 tablespoons dairy kefir grains

Instructions

1. Put the kefir grains in the quart jar and combine with the coconut milk. Stir the contents together.

2. Place the piece of cloth over the jar and adhere with a rubber band or piece of twine.

3. Allow to sit in a warm, undisturbed place for 24 to 48 hours.

4. When ready, strain with a fine strainer, and then bottle and refrigerate the liquid.

5. Save your strained kefir grains and use them to make a new batch.

Note: As stated earlier in this chapter, this method can be used to make a dairy alternative Kefir with any other nut- or seed-based milk. Coconut milk kefir has always been the favorite dairy alternative.

Flavoring Your Kefir

Similar to the recipes that I shared for kombucha, you can flavor your kefirs in two different ways. One method is to add your flavors directly to your kefir the way you might add cream and sugar to your coffee to enjoy it right away. Flavors like vanilla, cinnamon, cacao (raw unprocessed chocolate), honey, and various fruits like mangoes, berries, peaches can be added right away. They can be stirred in with a wooden spoon or placed in a blender with the kefir and blended. You can also add fruit to a second fermentation.

Milk Kefir: Second Fermentation

Similar to kombucha, you can flavor your kefir (both diary and non-dairy) by a second fermentation. I have found that adding ½ cup of fruit for every cup of kefir works great. Add the fruit to the kefir, stir it together, and let it sit out at room temperature for 24 hours. When it's ready, you can strain it or enjoy it as is. I like to make my second ferments by blending the fruit, spices, and various flavoring extracts with my prepared kefir in a blender. Once it's blended, I put it in jar, put a lid back on it, and let it sit on my counter for an additional 24 hours at room temperature.

Kefir Recipes

The following recipes can be made using either dairy or coconut milk kefir. I learned the art of kefir fermentation and smoothies from Nutritionist and Health and Wellness Coach Sarah Philip from *Abundelicious* (www.abundelicious.com). Sarah is a knowledgeable fermenter, gut healer, and motivator. The recipes in this section are courtesy of her and her vast knowledge of digestive health.

Each of these smoothies can be enjoyed immediately or they can be rebottled, sealed, and set on the counter for a second ferment. These are just a few examples of flavor blends that I have found that go really well together and that I enjoy. Other flavor combinations that you may want to play around with are maple and cinnamon, apple cinnamon, coffee, vanilla chai, pumpkin, pistachio, raisin, papaya, pineapple, cherry, and/or any variety of berries such as strawberry, raspberry, and blackberry.

Blueberry Kefir Smoothie

Ingredients
1 cup fresh or frozen blueberries
1 banana
1 cup homemade kefir (see page 83 or 90)
Optional: Additional water for thinning the recipe and a sweetening
   agent such as raw honey, agave, coconut nectar, or organic cane
   sugar

Instructions
1. Place all the ingredients in a blender and blend until smooth.
2. If you have thinner pourable kefir, this recipe makes a
    perfectly blended smoothie. If your kefir is thicker and
    chunkier, like yogurt, you will want to use the additional water
    to thin it out.

Mango Kefir "Lassie"

Ingredients

1 cup homemade kefir (see page 83 or 90)
1 banana
1 cup fresh or frozen mango
¼ teaspoon ground cardamom
Optional: Additional water for thinning the recipe and a sweetening
    agent such as raw honey, agave, coconut nectar, or organic cane
    sugar

Instructions

1. Place all the ingredients in a blender and blend until smooth.
2. If you have thinner, pourable kefir, this recipe makes a
   perfectly blended smoothie. If your kefir is thicker and
   chunkier, like yogurt, you will want to use the additional water
   to thin it out.

Peach, Matcha, and Basil Kefir Smoothie

Ingredients

1 cup homemade kefir (see pages 83 or 90)

1 banana

3 peaches or 1½ cups frozen peaches

½ cup orange juice

1 teaspoon matcha powder

2 tablespoons fresh basil (or 1 tablespoon dried basil)

1 tablespoon raw honey, agave, or coconut nectar

Instructions

1. Place all the ingredients in a blender and blend until smooth.
2. Garnish with a slice of peach and sprig of basil. Sip and enjoy!

Peach, Mango, Banana, Turmeric Kefir

Ingredients

1 cup homemade kefir (see pages 83 or 90)

1 banana

1 cup fresh or frozen mangoes

1 cup fresh or frozen peaches

1-inch piece of fresh turmeric (or 1 teaspoon of dried turmeric powder)

Optional: Additional water for thinning the recipe and a sweetening agent such as raw honey, agave, coconut nectar, or organic cane sugar

Instructions

1. Place all the ingredients in a blender and blend until smooth.
2. If you have thinner, pourable kefir, this recipe makes a perfectly blended smoothie. If your kefir is thicker and chunkier, like yogurt, you will want to use the additional water to thin it out.

The fruit profile in this smoothie tastes wonderful together. The turmeric gives this smoothie an amazingly bright yellow color. Turmeric is celebrated in the world of nutrition for having major benefits to your body and brain. It is highly anti-inflammatory, contains powerful antioxidants, and boosts brain function and longevity.

Chocolate Vanilla Kefir with Honey

Ingredients

1 cup homemade kefir (see pages 83 or 90)

2 tablespoons raw cacao powder

2 tablespoons raw unfiltered honey

½ teaspoon pure vanilla extract

3 bananas

¼ cup purified water

Optional: Additional water for thinning out the recipe

Instructions

1. Place all the ingredients in a blender and blend until smooth.
2. Cacao powder can act as a thickening agent. Depending on how pourable your kefir is, the combination of your cacao powder and kefir could make this smoothie very thick. Add additional water as needed.

CHAPTER 5
Rejuvelac

REJUVELAC IS A TART, FERMENTED beverage popular in the fermentation and health food community. It is celebrated for its probiotic, enzyme, vitamin, and mineral content. It can be enjoyed on its own, or it can be used as a fermentation starter or flavoring agent for other recipes. Rejuvelac is typically made from fermenting sprouted wheat berries. It can also be made using sprouted rye, sprouted buckwheat, sprouted quinoa, barley, oats, or rice. I enjoy making a sprouted grain blend using sprouted wheat, rye, oats, barley, buckwheat, and quinoa. Rejuvelac has an awakening lemony flavor and is very refreshing when combined with your favorite fruit juices and poured over ice. When I combine fruit juices to make rejuvelac "cocktails," I always use the ratio of 50% juice to 50% rejuvelac. As you already know, I strongly recommend using fresh fruit juice that you have made yourself. Adjust the recipes accordingly to fit your taste preferences.

Allergy Note: Anyone who has celiac disease or an extreme gluten sensitivity may want to avoid using wheat, rye, barley, or oats. In which case, you can just use buckwheat, quinoa, rice, or any combination of the three. Non-gluten containing seeds such as buckwheat and quinoa are called pseudograins (also in that category are amaranth and wild rice).

Wheat berries are the name for grains of wheat, or the seeds. Oat seeds are called oat groats, and buckwheat seeds are called buckwheat groats. For whatever reason quinoa, barley, and rye aren't lucky enough to get additional words of differentiation.

How to Make Rejuvelac

Ingredients

3 cups whole, raw wheat berries or any of the aforementioned grains
or pseudograins
1-gallon glass jar, jug, or crock
Purified water
Mesh or cheese cloth
Twine or a rubber band

Directions for sprouting wheat berries

1. Put 3 cups of wheat berries in a 1-gallon glass jar and fill to the top with water.
2. Allow the wheat berries to soak for 12 hours.
3. Adhere mesh or cheese cloth to the top of the jar and strain out the water.
4. Turn the jar on its side and allow wheat berries to spread evenly in the jar in order to get air.
5. Approximately twice a day or every 12 hours, turn the jar right-side up, fill the jar with water to rinse the wheat berries, and drain again.

6. Lay the jar back on its side.

7. In approximately 3 to 5 days, your wheat will germinate and grow sprouts.

Directions for making rejuvelac

1. Put your sprouted wheat berries in your 1-gallon glass jar, jug, or crock and fill to the top with purified water.

2. Adhere a piece of cloth, paper towel, or coffee filter to the top of the jug and put a rubber band around it.

3. Let the sprouts ferment for about 2 days at room temperature.

4. Taste test when you think it's ready. It should look cloudy and taste yeasty and lemony. There should be bubbles coming up from the fermenting grains at the bottom of the jar.

5. You can make a second batch from the sprouts, but the second time it will only take 24 hours to ferment.

Flavoring your Rejuvelac

When it comes to flavoring your rejuvelac after it has matured, there are many other options besides using only fruit juice. You can add raisins, dates, figs, or other dried or fresh fruits. I like adding herbal teas or mulling spices. When flavoring your rejuvelac with teas, add the tea bags to the batch after it has matured and before you place it in the refrigerator. Teas that I like to use as flavoring are: tangerine ginger, rooibos, hibiscus, mint, green, black, ginger, lemon, fruit teas, and flower teas such as marigold or rose (these are also wonderful teas to use for flavoring in the later chapter about lacto-fermented teas, page 119).

Since the recipe in this book shows you how to make 1 gallon of rejuvelac, you can divide your batch into smaller quart jars and flavor each one differently. I like to use 1 tea bag or 1 teaspoon of tea per 8 ounces of rejuvelac. Add your tea to your rejuvelac, put a lid on your jar, and place it in the refrigerator overnight.

Rejuvelac "Margarita"

This nonalcoholic concoction resembles a delicious and refreshing lemonade. The lemony flavor of the rejuvelac combines well with the lemon and lime juice. If your taste buds are still getting used to the flavor of rejuvelac, you may want to add more sweetener at first. Perhaps even a half cup. (Add jalapeños for an extra eye-popping zip!)

Equipment

Large pitcher or ½-gallon jar
Margarita glasses

Ingredients

½ cup fresh lemon juice
½ cup fresh lime juice
3 cups homemade rejuvelac (see page 104)
½ cup sliced fresh jalapeños
ice
Raw unfiltered honey, maple syrup, coconut nectar, or agave to taste
  (optional)

Instructions

1. In a large pitcher or ½ gallon mason jar, combine the jalapeños with the lemon juice, lime juice, and homemade rejuvelac. You could also add one of the suggested optional sweeteners at this time.
2. Stir them well with a wooden spoon.
3. Put ice in your glasses and fill with the rejuvelac margarita. Garnish with a lime.
4. Additional options: Add a dash of orange juice to mimic the flavor of triple sec, which is a prominent flavor in conventional margaritas. You can also salt the rim of your glasses to create a much more authentic margarita experience. Enjoy!

This recipe may be a little too tart and off-putting for some people's taste buds. Adding a little sweetness can brighten up the flavors and make this "margarita" and other rejuvelac mocktails more palatable. I suggest adding 1 to 2 teaspoons of one of the following sweeteners: honey, agave, coconut nectar, or maple syrup.

Rejuvelac Sangria

This is a healthy alcohol-free rendition of a Spanish favorite. This is a great recipe when entertaining guests who are health-conscious and would like to enjoy something that is celebratory and reminiscent of a cocktail. I encourage you to make the orange juice and the pineapple juice fresh. Okay, okay, since it's lacking red wine and brandy, it's nothing like true Spanish sangria, but it does create a very delicious and thirst-quenching juice cocktail that's great for entertaining.

Ingredients

2 cups rejuvelac (see page 104)
1 cup orange juice
1 cup pineapple juice
½ cup red grapes, halved
½ cup green grapes, halved
½ cup strawberries, halved
4 slices orange
4 slices lemon
4 slices lime

Instructions

1. In a large pitcher, combine the rejuvelac, orange juice, and pineapple juice.
2. Add the grapes, strawberries, oranges, lemons, and limes.
3. Stir the contents together.
4. Fill two pint classes with ice and pour the contents over it, ensuring that a generous amount of fruit gets into each glass. Garnish with a slice of lemon, lime, and/or orange on the rim of the glass.
5. Other fruit options that go well with this recipe are blueberries, raspberries, peaches, apples, pears, pineapple chunks, and slices of mango.

Pomegranate Rejuvelac

Rejuvelac goes very well when combined with many fruit juices, including pomegranate, at the 50/50 ratio. Orange, grapefruit, pineapple, strawberry, blueberry, and red grape juice all work well, too. Experiment in your kitchen and do what works for your taste preferences.

Ingredients

1 cup pomegranate juice
1 cup rejuvelac (see page 104)
ice

Instructions

1. Fill a pint glass or Collins glass with ice.
2. Combine the pomegranate juice and rejuvelac.
3. Garnish with a lemon or lime wedge and enjoy!

Vegan-Friendly Recipes Using Rejuvelac For Fermentation and Flavoring

When creating vegan delights that resemble dairy, you can use rejuvelac as your fermentation starter or flavoring agent. I was first turned on to rejuvelac as a means to make vegan cashew and almond yogurt. It can also be used to make nut-based sour cream, cheeses, or desserts like cheesecake. Not only does it add a slightly sour and delicious cheese flavoring, but it also boosts the nutritional profile of your creation/food by giving it a boost of probiotics, vitamin C, and B vitamins. Cashews, pine nuts, and macadamia nuts each blend very well to create the consistency of dairy products without using any actual dairy. Almonds also blend well when properly soaked, but they come with a fibrous outer brown layer that affects the texture of your recipe when blended together. It may feel a bit tedious, but if you desire a creamier texture with your almond-based recipes, remove the skin with your fingers after soaking.

Cashew Yogurt Using Rejuvelac

Equipment
High-powered blender or a food processor

Ingredients
1¼ cups cashews, soaked for 1 hour

2 tablespoons lemon juice

1 tablespoon homemade rejuvelac (see page 104)

⅛ teaspoon sea salt

½ teaspoon pure vanilla extract

½ cup purified water

Raw unfiltered honey, maple syrup, or agave, to taste. (Optional: This can be added if you prefer a sweeter yogurt.)

Instructions
1. Put all ingredients (including optional sweeteners) in the blender or food processor (fitted with the S blade) and blend until smooth.
2. Place the yogurt in a bowl, cover with a piece of cloth or towel, and set in a warm, undisturbed area for 12 hours.
3. Taste your yogurt and add additional sweetener or fresh fruit to fit your taste preferences. Similar to kefir, fresh fruits such as berries, mangoes, and peaches go very well with cashew yogurt.
4. Enjoy right away or refrigerate and eat later. Will keep in the refrigerator for up to 5 days.

Almond Yogurt Using Rejuvelac

Equipment
High-powered blender or a food processor

Ingredients
1¼ cups almonds, soaked for 24 hours

2 tablespoons lemon juice

1 tablespoon homemade rejuvelac (see page 104)

⅛ teaspoon sea salt

½ teaspoon pure vanilla extract

½ cup purified water

Raw unfiltered honey, maple syrup, or agave to taste. (Optional. This can be added if you prefer a sweeter yogurt.)

Instructions
1. Put all ingredients in the blender or food processor (fitted with the S blade) and blend until smooth.
2. Place the yogurt in a bowl, cover with a piece of cloth or towel, and set in a warm, undisturbed area for 12 hours.
3. Taste your yogurt and add additional sweetener or fresh fruit to fit your taste preferences. Similar to kefir, fresh fruits such as berries, mangoes, and peaches go very well with cashew yogurt.
4. Enjoy right away or refrigerate and consume later. Will keep in the refrigerator for up to 5 days.

Non-Dairy Raw Sour "Cream"

Equipment
High-powered bender

Ingredients
1½ cups cashews, soaked for 1 hour
½ cup water
½ teaspoon sea salt
2 tablespoons lemon juice
1 tablespoon homemade rejuvelac (page 104)

Instructions
1. Blend all ingredients in a blender until smooth and creamy. The combination of rejuvelac and lemon juice makes this recipe taste strikingly similar to dairy-based sour cream. To sour it up even more and increase the friendly bacteria content, cover with a cloth and leave it sit out at room temperature for an additional 12 hours. Add this recipe to a baked potato or vegetarian tacos!

Non-Dairy Raw Ranch Dressing

Equipment
High-powered blender

Ingredients
1½ cups cashews or macadamia nuts

½ cup water

3 tablespoons lemon juice

2 tablespoons rejuvelac

1–2 cloves garlic

1–2 teaspoons sea salt

½ teaspoon dried dill

½ teaspoon dried basil

1 stalk celery

Instructions
1. Place all ingredients in a blender and process until smooth and creamy. Add less water for a dip. Add more water for a dressing.
2. Once it has been inoculated with the rejuvelac, it has become probiotic. It can be enjoyed as is or, for a second fermentation, cover the dressing with a towel or a piece of cloth and allow to sit undisturbed at room temperature for an additional 12 hours.

CHAPTER 6
Probiotic Drinks

Ginger Beer, Ginger Ale, Lacto-fermented Sodas, and Beyond!

Making fizzy, probiotic, lacto-fermented ales, sodas, and teas allows us nearly endless possibilities. As I stated in the Kombucha chapter, your only limitations are your own creativity. Lacto-fermented sodas and teas are created by adding sugar and flavoring in the way of herbal teas or fruit juice (or both!) to water and starter culture. Allow them to sit and ferment, and you have a fizzy and refreshing finished product with probiotic and nutritional benefits.

The recipes in this chapter are for making a quart of fermentation at a time. In almost all the other chapters, I've shown you how to make 1 gallon of fermentations such as kombucha and rejuvelac. Both kombucha and rejuvelac can be enjoyed daily in sizable quantities as is or used to make an endless variety of other tasty beverages. You may want to make a large quantity of lacto-fermented teas and sodas. Knowing how to make them 1 quart at a time gives you the freedom to make multiple batches of different flavors and varieties. One cup of starter culture from water kefir or leftover whey can be used to make three or four new batches of fizzy, lacto-fermented drinks.

In this chapter, I teach you how to make water kefir as a delicious fizzy drink and a starter liquid to create your fermented teas and sodas. Water kefir has no dairy in it and is not the same as dairy kefir, which we learned about in chapter 4. To make water kefir you need a different kind of kefir grains called water kefir grains. Self-explanatory right? Water kefir grains are not actual grains at all, which means they are gluten free and do not contain any other nutrients or allergens that one might associate with grains. Water kefir grains are small, rubbery cell structures that resemble tiny cauliflower florets and are made from a combination of bacteria and yeast.

Similar to your kombucha scoby, water kefir grains feed on sugar. You can purchase water kefir grains at some health-food stores or online. Water kefir grains can also be gifted to you by someone who makes water kefir at home. As I stated earlier in the dairy kefir chapter, there are meet-up groups, fermentation clubs, and online chat forums where people are usually willing to give water kefir grains to fermentation enthusiasts.

Ginger Ale versus Ginger Beer

Many people discuss "ginger ale" and "ginger beer" as though they're the same beverage, and they're not. "Ginger beer" is a unique brew that is fermented for 2 to 3 weeks and requires a very specific starter called a "ginger bug" to initiate fermentation. "Ginger ale" can be made a number of ways. It can be created by brewing a lacto-fermented tea with water kefir, whey, or a powdered starter culture (you will learn more about this later in this chapter). Another common way people make ginger ale is simply combining ginger flavoring, sugar, and carbonated water.

Ginger beer requires something called a "ginger bug" for a starter. Making ginger beer is a three-step process that may seem a bit tedious, but it's well worth it. You begin by making a ginger bug. Then you ferment your brew by using water, sugar, and lemon juice. Finally, you bottle it and allow it to sit undisturbed for a second fermentation. Ginger bug isn't something you can borrow from a friend, buy at a health-food store, or purchase online. You have to make it yourself in your kitchen.

I have included a few of my favorite recipes here. As you may be aware, ginger is an incredibly delicious and versatile spice. It can be used for both sweet and savory dishes and it goes well with a plethora of different fruits. Ginger plays the leading role in favorite sweets like gingerbread cookies, and it is also the primary flavor alongside garlic in gourmet Thai dishes such as Tom Yum and Coconut Curry. There are so many delicious flavors you can add above and beyond what I have included here. Orange, pineapple, basil, peach, cherry, grape, coconut, vanilla, cinnamon, and cardamom are just a few. Enjoy experimenting!

Ginger Bug

Equipment

1-quart glass jar
Piece of cloth, paper towel, or coffee filter
Rubber band
1-gallon jar or jug

Ingredients

2 tablespoons grated fresh ginger per day (10 tablespoons total)
2 tablespoons raw organic sugar per day (10 tablespoons total)
1 cup purified water

Instructions

1. Start your ginger bug by adding 2 tablespoons of grated ginger to 2 tablespoons of sugar in your quart jar.
2. Add 1 cup purified water.
3. Cover the jar with a piece of cloth, paper towel, or coffee filter and adhere with a rubber band.
4. Allow jar to sit in a warm, undisturbed area for 24 hours.
5. Every day for the next 4 days, add 2 tablespoons of grated ginger, 2 tablespoons of sugar, and 2 tablespoons of purified water. Stir at least twice a day.
6. After a total of 5 days, your ginger bug should be bubbly and smell a little yeasty, like beer.
7. Place your ginger bug in the fridge. It's now ready to be used to make ginger beer. Only the liquid from the ginger bug is used to make ginger beer, so you will need to strain it off before using. As you continue to use liquid from your ginger bug, you will want to top up your ginger bug with more ginger, sugar, and water.

Ginger Beer

My goal was to give you a recipe that you could follow as easily as possible. It will make just slightly more than a quart. Ginger beer can keep in the fridge for up to 1 month.

Equipment

1-quart glass jar
Piece of cloth, paper towel, or coffee filter
Rubber band
½-gallon jar or jug

Ingredients

¼ cup sugar
⅛ cup lemon juice
1½ tablespoons fresh grated ginger
¼ cup ginger bug liquid (see page 122)
1 quart purified water

Instructions

1. In your ½-gallon jar or jug, combine the sugar, lemon juice, fresh grated ginger, ginger bug, and water. Stir well.
2. Cover the jar with a piece of cloth, paper towel, or coffee filter and adhere with a rubber band.
3. Place in a warm, dark area for 7 to 10 days. Stir it once or twice a day.
4. Sample it. It should taste slightly fizzy and there should be large bubbles forming on the surface.
5. If it doesn't taste sweet any longer, that means the microbes consumed all the sugar. You may have to add 1 to 2 more tablespoons of sugar. Depending on the flavor, you may also want to add more grated ginger. This is essential to the second fermentation.
6. Now you are ready to bottle the ginger beer as it is, or flavor it for a second fermentation.

7. If bottling as it is, pour the liquid into sealable bottles and place in a warm, dark place for 2 to 4 days. This process makes the ginger beer very carbonated and, if left out at room temperature for too long, the bottle might combust. The level of sweetness, fizziness, and ginger flavor are all a matter of your taste preference. Keep experimenting until you find the exact balance that you enjoy.

8. Place the bottles in the refrigerator to slow the fermentation. The ginger beer will continue to ferment in the refrigerator, so it will be important to open bottles slowly, pointing away from your face.

Strawberry Rosemary Ginger Beer

Strawberry and ginger go incredibly well together. Strawberry ginger beer is my favorite of all second-fermentation flavors. In this recipe, I add some rosemary, which gives this a piney and woody herbal enhancement. Rosemary can easily overpower a recipe. The goal is for there to be subtle flavor of rosemary to complement the ginger and strawberries but not too strong. This is a very refreshing beverage that goes well with an additional squeeze of lemon.

Ingredients

1 cup fresh, ripe strawberries, chopped or pulsed in a food processor
2 tablespoons fresh rosemary
1 tablespoon sugar
4 cups homemade ginger beer (see page 124)

Instructions

1. In a glass jug or ½-gallon jar, combine the strawberries, rosemary, sugar, and homemade ginger beer.
2. Stir until the sugar is dissolved and the other ingredients are well blended.
3. Divide the contents between two sealable quart jars. Seal tight and leave out at room temperature for 2 to 4 days.
4. When ready to drink, put in the refrigerator for 1 hour to slow down the fermentation before opening.
5. Strain out the rosemary and strawberry pulp or enjoy as is.

"Moscow Mule" with Cucumber and Mint

This is nonalcoholic rendition of a timeless favorite. A Moscow mule is typically made with vodka and limes, and the mixing agent that gives it its signature flavor is ginger beer. The cucumber and lime add an extra-refreshing infusion. With this recipe, I add an extra tablespoon of sugar since there is very little sugar in the mint, lime, and cucumber for the microbes to feed off.

Ingredients

4 cups homemade ginger beer (see page 124)

2 tablespoons sugar

2 tablespoons fresh-squeezed lime juice

¼ cup chopped fresh mint

½ cup sliced cucumbers

Instructions

1. In a large jar or jug, combine the ginger beer, sugar, lime juice, mint leaves, and cucumbers.

2. Stir until the sugar is dissolved and the contents are well mixed.

3. Divide the mixture into two quart-sized sealable jars. Seal tight and place in a warm, dark place for 2 to 4 days.

4. When ready to drink, put in the refrigerator for 1 hour to slow down the fermentation.

5. Strain out the mint and lime juice pulp or enjoy as is.

Water Kefir

Water kefir is a dairy-free and vegan-friendly probiotic drink that can be easily made at home using sugar, water, and kefir grains. Water kefir grains are clear and resemble tiny bubbles or "grains." They are also referred to as tibi crystals, tibicos, Japanese water crystals, Japanese beer seeds, sugar kefir grains, and California bees. Similar to dairy kefir, water kefir is very easy to make and involves minimal ingredients. Aside from being a healthy probiotic drink, water kefir is rich in enzymes and minerals, making it a beneficial electrolyte sports drink. The second fermentation is flavored and creates the lacto-fermented tea or "soda" explained earlier in this chapter.

Water kefir grains can also be used to make coconut water kefir from young coconuts. Coconut water kefir creates a fizzy probiotic beverage that resembles champagne and of course has a pleasant coconut flavor.

Water Kefir

Equipment

½-gallon glass jar or jug

Wooden spoon

Fine strainer

Piece of cloth, paper towel, or
coffee filter

Rubber band

Ingredients

¼ cup sugar

1 cup hot water

4 cups room-temperature water

¼ cup hydrated water kefir grains

Instructions

1. Dissolve the ¼ cup of sugar in 1 cup of hot water.
2. Combine the sugar-water with the 4 cups of room-temperature water in a ½-gallon glass jar or jug.
3. Allow to cool. The water must be cooled down or you risk it killing the probiotics in your kefir grains.
4. Mix in your kefir grains and stir well.
5. Cover with a piece of cloth, paper towel, or coffee filter and place in an undisturbed area for 2 to 3 days. When it's ready, it should have a lemony and yeasty scent and there should be foam or small bubbles on the surface.
6. Once your water kefir is ready, it can be consumed as is or you can use it to make a second fermentation. Strain out your kefir grains and put them aside for your next batch. You can use the same kefir grains an unlimited number of times as long as you feed them and keep them healthy.

Storing your water kefir grains: If you do not want to make a continuous brew of water kefir, you will want to properly store your kefir grains. They will thrive best in a sugar-water solution. In a quart jar, dissolve ¼ cup of sugar in 1 quart of purified water. Put your kefir grains in the jar and seal the lid. Place in the refrigerator. Ideally, you'll want to change out the sugar-water each week. The kefir grains will be safe and healthy for up to 3 weeks.

Making "Soda" and Bubbly Fermented Teas

Lacto-fermented Sodas

Making homemade sodas is a way of turning your favorite fruits and fruit juices into bubbly, fizzy soda-like beverages. If you're a chronic soda-drinker and you're looking for a healthy alternative, these recipes are a great way to curb your unhealthy habit. I've also heard from mothers who have said that their children love these recipes since they resemble classic fruit-flavored sodas but without the syrupy sweetness. Well, moms, unlike commercial sodas, these fizzy beverages contain enzymes, probiotics, and actual nutrients. Some lacto-fermented sodas work better with whole fruit and others work better with fruit juice. Always use 100% fruit juice and, as you already know, I swear by making fresh juice yourself for these recipes. Your ferments will be more nutritious if you use unpasteurized juice that you've made yourself, and, not to mention, more flavorful.

When using juice, the general rule is 1 cup of fresh 100% juice to 4 cups of homemade water kefir. Different fruits naturally have different sugar contents and, as a result, will ferment at different speeds. I have learned that some fruits work better juiced, while other fruits work better whole or slightly chopped or pureed. Included here are some of my favorite lacto-fermented fruit-based sodas.

Raspberry Soda

This is a huge crowd favorite. Nothing beats real raspberry soda made from fresh raspberries. The color and flavor are reminiscent of conventional sodas but way healthier and refreshing. I also love making blueberry, strawberry, blackberry, or a mixed berry combination. A favorite among children and families.

Ingredients

2 cups raspberries

¼ cup sugar

½ cup warm water

4 cups homemade water kefir (page 131)

4 cups purified water

Instructions

1. Put the raspberries in a blender and puree briefly.
2. Dissolve the ¼ cup of sugar in ½ cup of warm water (allow to cool before combing it with your water kefir).
3. In a large jar or pitcher, combine the water kefir, raspberry puree, and sugar-water.
4. Pour the contents into 2 sealable quart-sized jars and tightly seal.
5. Leave in a warm, dark place for 1 to 2 days.
6. Point away from your face and open slowly. Strain out the contents or enjoy as is.

Cranberry Orange Soda

When I originally included this recipe, I was only going to show you how to make classic orange soda (which doesn't taste anything like real oranges) from fresh-squeezed orange juice. This book is designed to encourage you to be creative, and I find unsweetened cranberry juice to complement this recipe quite well. Make it unique and even more delicious by spicing it up with cardamom, clove, cinnamon, or a combination of mulling spices.

Ingredients

¼ cup sugar

½ cup hot water

4 cups homemade water kefir (page 131)

1 cup freshly squeezed orange juice

½ cup unsweetened cranberry juice, preferably homemade

Instructions

1.   Dissolve the sugar in the warm water (allow to cool down before combining it with your water kefir).
2.   In a large jar or pitcher, combine the water kefir, orange juice, cranberry juice, and sugar-water.
3.   Pour the contents into 2 sealable quart-sized jars and tightly seal.
4.   Leave in a warm, dark place for 1 to 2 days.
5.   Point away from your face and open slowly. Strain out the pulp or enjoy as is.

Peach Soda

I love the flavor of anything with peach in it, and nothing creates a nostalgic summer flavor like a recipe made with ripe, seasonal peaches. Fruits like peaches, pears, and mangoes don't juice as well as other fruits do. When peaches are put through a juicer, they make more of a "nectar." This recipes calls for whole peaches chopped up. I don't even strain out my peaches when I make this brew. I encourage you to enjoy as is!

Ingredients

½ cup hot water
¼ cup sugar
4 cups homemade water kefir (page 131)
2 large ripe peaches, pitted and chopped

Instructions

1. Dissolve the sugar in the warm water (allow to cool down before combining it with your water kefir).
2. In a large jar or pitcher, combine the water kefir, chopped peaches, and sugar-water. Stir well.
3. Pour the contents into 2 sealable quart-sized jars and tightly seal.
4. Leave in a warm, dark place for 1 to 2 days.
5. Point away from your face and open slowly. Strain out the pieces of peach or enjoy as is.

Lemon-Lime Soda

In many fermentation books, entire chapters are dedicated to lemon-based fermentations. Lacto-fermented lemonade, lemon soda, lemon kombucha, and kefir lemonade are all probiotic favorites. Lemon goes extraordinarily well with other citrus fruits, berries, ginger, and hot peppers. This recipe shows you how to create a healthy parody on Sprite and 7Up: a thirst-quenching and hydrating lemon-lime probiotic soda.

Ingredients

¼ sugar

½ cup hot water

4 cups homemade water kefir (page 131)

¼ cup lemon juice

¼ cup lime juice

Instructions

1. Dissolve the sugar in the warm water (allow to cool down before combining it with your water kefir).
2. In a large jar or pitcher, combine the water kefir, lemon juice, lime juice, and sugar-water. Stir well.
3. Pour the contents into 2 sealable quart-sized jars and tightly seal.
4. Leave in a warm, dark place for 1 to 2 days.
5. Point away from your face and open slowly. Enjoy as is, or pour over ice like lemonade and garnish with a lime or lemon.

Lacto-fermented Herbal Tea

People drink tea for many different reasons. As I discussed in the kombucha chapter, technically a "tea" is only made from the *Camellia sinensis* plant. Green, white, black, yellow, pu-erh, and oolong are all varieties of caffeinated tea that come from different plants in the *Camellia sinensis* family. Herbal teas, or "tisanes," are made from steeping non-caffeinated herbs, flowers, and fruits in hot water to make a healthy or flavorful infusion. When it comes to making fermented teas, there are so many possibilities. Are you looking for something that has therapeutic properties such as nettle, dandelion, red raspberry leaf, or milk thistle? Or are you looking to brew something that has an invigorating taste and wakes up the senses like rose, orange peel, clove, or ginger? Fermenting herbal teas is a way of turning your favorite herbal blends into delicious, fizzy refreshments. Some of my favorites herbal teas to use in creating second fizzy ferments from a batch of water kefir are elderberry, marigold, goji berry, ginger, yerba mate, lemongrass, and rooibos.

The herbalists, healers, and wellness experts at MKE Mind Body Wellness (www.mkewellness.com) helped me formulate the recipes in this section for fermenting teas. At MKE Mind Body Wellness, they focus on good health for the mainstream, which means their food and beverages MUST taste good. The owners, Jonathan and

Aleisha Anderson, love experimenting with the medicinal plant kava as a tea and fermentation. Kava is a slightly bitter-tasting root native to the Polynesian islands that is highly celebrated for its medicinal properties. It is used to calm anxiety, stress, restlessness, and to treat insomnia. When you combine the stress-reducing properties of kava with the brain chemistry balancing properties of the probiotic drink, you create a very therapeutic health tonic. Since kava can have a strong, off-putting flavor, Jonathan and Aleisha like to brew it with rose, lemon peel, orange peel, cinnamon, or ginger.

Ingredients
4 cups purified water
¼ cup loose herbal tea or 4 tea bags
¼ cup sugar
¼ cup homemade water kefir (page 131)

Instructions
1. Place the 4 cups of water over high heat and bring almost to a boil.
2. Stir in your herbal tea, cover, and let steep for at least 10 minutes. This will help extract the properties of the herbs.
3. Strain the tea from the herbs into another quart jar. Add sugar while the tea is still hot in order to properly mix and dissolve the sugars.
4. Allow to cool to room temperature. When the tea has cooled, stir in the homemade water kefir.
5. Pour the contents into a quart jar and cover with a piece of cloth, paper towel, or coffee filter.
6. Leave in a warm, dark place for 2 to 4 days.
7. Strain out the tea and pour into 2 glass quart-sized jars.

Second Ferment
Once the tea has been strained out, it is now ready for the second fermentation, which will allow your lacto-fermented tea to become fizzy and bubbly.

Add ½ teaspoon of sugar to each jar and seal tight. Let the bottles sit at room temperature for 1 to 2 days before drinking. From the second fermentation, you should have a pleasantly bubbly brew infused with your favorite herbal tea.

Ginger Ale

Even though it is thought of as a soda, traditionally ginger ale is one of the most popular lacto-fermented teas. It is essentially a second fermentation of water kefir crafted by fermenting a strong ginger tea.

Ingredients

4 cups purified water

4 inches ginger root, peeled and grated

¾ cup sugar

1 cup homemade water kefir (page 131)

Instructions

1. Place the 4 cups of water over high heat and stir in the ginger root. Bring the water to a boil and boil for 3 minutes.

2. Stir in the sugar until it dissolves, and let it cool until room temperature. When sufficiently cool, stir in water kefir.

3. Pour into a ½-gallon glass jar or jug.

4. Cover with a piece of cloth, paper towel, or coffee filter. Adhere with a rubber band.

5. Keep at room temperature or 2 to 6 days, until the ginger ale is fizzy. Strain out the piece of ginger root at this time.

6. Bottle in tightly capped beverage bottles and let sit at room temperature for 1 to 2 days before drinking.

Coconut Water Kefir

Coconut water kefir can be made the exact same way as the recipe for water kefir on page 131. One exception is that you don't need to add sugar to coconut water kefir if you don't want to. There is enough naturally occurring sugar in coconut water to allow it to ferment in 24 hours. The benefit of adding ¼ cup of sugar to coconut water kefir is that it makes it extra tangy, fizzy, and abundant in probiotics.

Equipment

½-gallon glass jar or jug
wooden spoon
fine strainer
piece of cloth, paper towel, or coffee filter
rubber band

Ingredients

¼ cup sugar
4 cups coconut water
¼ cup hydrated water kefir grains

Instructions

1. In a ½-gallon glass jar or jug, dissolve the ¼ cup of sugar in 4 cups of coconut water.
2. Mix in your kefir grains and stir well.
3. Cover with a piece of cloth, paper towel, or coffee filter and place in an undisturbed area for 2 to 3 days. When it's ready, you should have a delicious fizzy drink that resembles coconut champagne.
4. Once your coconut water kefir is ready, it can be consumed as is or you can use it to make a second fermentation. Tropical fruits such as mango, papaya, pineapple, guava, and passion fruit pair nicely with coconut. Come to think of it, I've never tried a single fruit that doesn't go well with coconut water kefir. This is why I love using coconut water kefir as the base for my morning smoothies.

Coconut Water Kefir Smoothies

My favorite way to enjoy coconut kefir is as a base for smoothies. Many smoothie recipes call for juice, milk, yogurt, or just plain water. You can substitute coconut kefir for any conventional liquid that a smoothie recipe may call for. I encourage you to add a ¼ cup of coconut or dairy kefir as well to really flavor up your smoothies and to pack a probiotic punch. My introduction to the world of green and superfood smoothies came from certified aroma therapist, cancer survivor, healer, and superfood expert Pat Molter (www.patmolter. com). She inspired me to write the following recipes.

Emerald City

Ingredients

2 bananas

1 orange

1 cup pineapple

1 cup spinach

1 cup coconut water kefir (see page 147)

½ cup dairy or coconut kefir (see page 83 or 90) (optional)

Instructions

1. Place all of the ingredients in a high-powered blender and blend until smooth. The spinach gives this smoothie a vibrant green color.

2. Optional: Add ½ cup of dairy or coconut kefir for a concoction that looks and tastes more like a piña colada.

Banana Egg-less Nog

Ingredients

½ cup pecans, soaked

3 bananas

2 dates, pitted

½ teaspoon pure vanilla extract

¼ teaspoon ground cinnamon

⅛ teaspoon ground nutmeg

pinch of ground cloves

pinch of sea salt

1½ cups coconut water kefir (see page 147)

½ cup dairy or coconut kefir (see page 83 or 90) (optional)

Instructions

1. Place all ingredients in a blender and blend until smooth.
2. Add dairy or coconut kefir to this recipe for an extra thick and creamy blended drink.

Brain Berry Madness

Ingredients

2 cups fresh or frozen mixed berries (blueberries, raspberries, blackberries, and strawberries are a good blend. All good brain food!)

2 bananas

1 cup kale

1 tablespoon raw unfiltered honey, maple syrup, agave, or coconut nectar

1 cup homemade coconut water kefir (see page 147)

Instructions

1. Place all ingredients in a high-powered blender and blend until smooth. The unique nutrition profile from the berries, kale, and kefir make this blend super brain food!

Breakfast Smoothie

Ingredients

½ cup old-fashioned oats

2 bananas

1 cup kefir (dairy or coconut, see page 83 or 90)

½ cup coconut water kefir (see page 147)

1 tablespoon maple syrup

1 teaspoon pure vanilla extract

1 teaspoon ground cinnamon

⅛ teaspoon sea salt

Instructions

1. Place all ingredients in a blender and blend until smooth.

2. To really make this hearty fast-breaker wake you up and prepare you for the day, swap the coconut water kefir for a half-full cup of coffee. Depending on your taste preferences, you may need to increase the maple syrup. Enjoy! Seize the day!

CHAPTER 7
Kvass and Fermented Vegetable Juices

KVASS IS A FIZZY BREAD drink consumed in Russia and other Slavic countries dating back to ancient times. Some say it was invented by mistake after a bag of grain was left out and got wet. The grain started to grow, and it was no longer usable to make bread. Water was added, it fermented, and thus, the first ever kvass was created. The main ingredient of true kvass is rye bread, even though the home ferment and the recipes in this book are made from fruits and vegetables (primarily beets). Kvass has a high content of B vitamins and is known to be an energy booster. It is reported that it was touted so much as a health aid that people would bathe in it. Even an ancient Russian saying declares, "Bad kvass is better than good water." As stated above kvass, is typically made from fermenting bread, raisins, and other dried fruit.

This recipes in this book is made from beets, which makes it gluten free and incredibly nutrient dense. I have heard fellow authors and fermentation enthusiasts refer to beet kvass as being the "King of all Ferments." In her book *Delicious Probiotic Drinks*, Julia Mueller says the beet kvass is "arguably the most nutrient dense and beneficial drink" in her whole book. Beets truly are an amazing vegetable. Not only are they delicious both cooked, raw, and pickled, but they are incredibly healthy and easy to include in your diet. Beets are high in vitamin C and loaded with the minerals manganese, magnesium, phosphorous, potassium, and iron. Beets are known for lowering blood pressure, and boosting energy and stamina, and are a great for cardiovascular health.

There are many unique recipes in the fermentation world to make beet kvass. Some include red cabbage, horseradish, turnips, ginger, onion, garlic, carrots, and mustard seeds. Some recipes suggest adding ¼ cup of whey or juice from a batch of fermented vegetables such as sauerkraut or kimchi. While these are all good suggestions for starter cultures and provide a culinary enthusiast with endless ideas for experimentation, I have included a very basic beet kvass recipe. Raw beets have all the necessary bacteria to get this beverage fermenting. Like almost every other recipe in this book, the length of time depends on temperature, ratio of ingredients, ecology of microbes, and flavor preferences. The recipe that I have included here is made from beets, water, and sea salt, but I encourage you to let your ideas run wild with any of the aforementioned extracurricular ingredients.

Beet Kvass Recipe

As stated earlier, the length of time you'll allow this drink to ferment depends on many factors, including your taste preferences. Kvass can be an acquired taste for some people. If you don't enjoy drinking it directly, you can use it for soups like borscht or gazpacho or as a base for salad dressings. Once your taste buds come around to enjoying kvass, you will enjoy experimenting with the herbs and seasonings discussed earlier. I always include a thumb-sized piece of ginger in my kvass, because I include ginger in almost every recipe. My hometown drinks a lot of Bloody Marys, and a spicy beet kvass made with cayenne pepper, ginger, garlic, and onion is a delicious addition to a Bloody Mary recipe.

Equipment
½-gallon sized jar
piece of cloth, paper towel, or coffee filter
rubber band
wooden spoon

Ingredients
1 large beet
1 tablespoon sea salt
4 cups purified water

Instructions
1. Clean the beet very well and slice into ½-inch squares.
2. Put the beet in the ½-gallon jar and add the purified water.
3. Stir in the sea salt.
4. Screw on a lid and let it sit on your counter for 4 to 14 days. Unscrew the lid briefly to "burp" the Kvass every 2 days.
5. Shake or stir the contents every day. This is essential because mold may form on the top. *What mold?* you're thinking. Yes, sometimes mold forms on the top of kvass and other vegetable

Continued on page 160

ferments. The truth is that, below the surface where the beets have been fermenting anaerobically (without oxygen), the environment does not support the growth of mold. The combination of salt and beneficial microbes in your kvass will prevent it from molding if it is stirred or shaken regularly. Many recipes for making kvass state that if mold or gray foam appear on the top, you can simply scoop it off and keep fermenting.

6. Strain out the liquid and enjoy. The beets can be eaten or discarded. I like to put them on my salads. Your kvass will taste sour and slightly effervescent.

Orange Carrot Ginger Kvass

Orange carrot ginger juice is delicious. Orange carrot ginger soup, both hot and cold, is also delicious. This is the close fermented cousin of this delectable holy trinity of culinary flavors. It can be made even more tangy and effervescent if you add a small amount of honey, or other sweetener, and bottle it for a second fermentation. I make this recipe nearly the same as the beet version. I just add ginger and orange peel. Similar to beet kvass, some fermentation enthusiasts swear by adding whey as a starter or liquid from a previously matured ferment such as sauerkraut or kimchi.

Ingredients

5–6 large carrots (about 3 cups), cut into small ½-inch pieces
2 (1-inch) pieces ginger, chopped into small pieces (about
   2 tablespoons)
entire peel of 1 organic orange, sliced or cut into chunks
1 tablespoon sea salt
4 cups purified water

Instructions

1. Put the carrots, ginger, orange peel, and sea salt into a ½-gallon jar and stir well.

2. Add the water and cover tightly with a lid.

3. Allow to sit on the counter for 4 to 14 days. It will continue to get more and more sour the longer it ferments.

4. Shake the contents daily or stir the liquid to prevent mold.

5. Every 2 days, unscrew the cap briefly to release built-up gas.

6. When ready, strain out the carrot, ginger, and orange peel and enjoy.

Full disclosure: This recipe tastes vastly different from traditional orange carrot ginger juice or soup. Once you build up your fermentation pallet, you'll find it fragrant, spicy, and delicious. If interested in a sweeter, bubblier brew, pour the contents into sealable quart jars, add a ½ teaspoon of sugar or honey, seal tight, and leave undisturbed on your counter for a few days. The result will be a slightly sweeter and fizzier version. Remember to open the bottle slowly and point away from your face.

Fruit Kvass

Fruit Kvass is one of simplest and easiest recipes in this book that has the most crowd appeal. Of course, it has the fizzy and sour flavor typical of a fruit-based ferment, but I think it's the fact that it tastes like a cider that makes it such a favorite. You can use nearly any fruit you want as long as it has a moderate sugar content (technically avocados and cucumbers are fruits, but they have little sugar content). Similar to many of the other fermentations in this book, Fruit Kvass encourages experimentation. Fruit Kvass can be made with many creative and unique combinations of fruits and spices. Peach blackberry, nectarine cardamom, apple cinnamon, mint lime, ginger apricot, cherry vanilla, and lemon ginger are all some fun ideas to play with. Raisins, figs, dried prunes, dried apricots, mint, lemon balm, lemongrass, and basil are all potential flavoring agents, as well. To inoculate your brew and accelerate the fermentation, you can add a small amount of fermentation starter, such as whey, or ½ cup of mature kombucha.

Ingredients

2 cups of your favorite fruit, chopped up into ½-inch pieces
4 cups purified water
½ teaspoon sea salt
1 tablespoon honey

Instructions

1. Combine all ingredients in a ½-gallon jar, and mix well to properly dissolve the honey and sea salt. You may need to dissolve some honey in ½ cup of warm water first.
2. Cover tight and allow the contents to sit on the counter for 4 to 14 days.
3. Shake the contents daily or stir the liquid to prevent mold.
4. Every 2 days, unscrew the cap briefly to release built-up gas.
5. After 2 days, you can begin to sample it daily. The longer you let it sit, the more sour it will get. You know when Fruit Kvass is done when your fruit looks "cooked" and your brew is bubbly.
6. Strain out the contents or enjoy as is.

CHAPTER 8
Superfoods

ASIDE FROM THE DIGESTIVE BENEFITS of probiotic foods, you also put nutrients from quality whole foods in your body. Some might argue that probiotic drinks are superfoods. In David Wolfe's book titled *Superfoods*, he refers to these nutrient dense foods and herbs as having the highest concentration of proteins, minerals, antioxidants, good fats and oils, essential amino acids, glyconutrients, vitamins, essential fatty acids, enzymes, coenzymes, and polysaccharides. Similar to categorical "superfoods," probiotic beverages are loaded with health-promoting nutrition, as well: a full spectrum of friendly microorganisms, vitamin C, minerals, enzymes, B vitamins, beneficial acids, and alkalizing properties. Probiotic drinks also contain immunity boosting and anti-inflammatory compounds. From my study of nutritional herbology and ethnobotany over the years, I have found that many superfoods, herbs, and teas are excellent complements to fermenting probiotic drinks. Many of them I have already included in the different recipes through this book.

In the same way that uninformed scientists gave all bacteria a bad rap, food has been misunderstood and mislabeled in a similar manner. We now live in the age of "nutritionism," a word made popular by journalist and health writer Michael Pollen. Nutritionism is the belief that food is no more beneficial than the sum of its parts. It is the ideology that food is strictly a vehicle to deliver certain isolated nutrients into the body and there is little value in the actual food itself. Allopathic doctors and natural health practitioners alike are prescribing patients a menagerie of candy-colored vitamin isolates and mineral supplements in an attempt to rebalance their over-toxic, undernourished bodies. Vitamin C, digestive enzymes, B-complex, GABA, probiotics, iron, calcium, magnesium, selenium, glucosamine, and omega-3 EPA/DHA are just a few of the ones that I am commonly asked about. I kindly remind people that our bodies do not efficiently digest and assimilate laboratory-fabricated chemical-isolated compact nutrients. Our bodies efficiently digest, absorb, and assimilate whole food. **EAT FOOD**. Whole, raw, organic, non-genetically modified(GMO), plant-based food.

The truth is that food is not just the sum of its parts. There is a nearly incomprehensible synergy of chemicals, nutrients, water, and fiber working together in our food that allows us to efficiently utilize it for optimal health. To list a few examples; in order to absorb calcium efficiently, our bodies need vitamin D, vitamin K, magnesium, and zinc. To better absorb our essential fatty acids (such as the omega-3 EFA), our bodies need vitamin C, a complete profile of B vitamins, zinc, and magnesium. To properly absorb vitamin C, we need vitamin E, vitamin A, and bioflavonoids.

The plus side of the age of Nutritionism is that doctors, scientists, and nutritionists are deeply fascinated with and committed to exploring the depths of our foods' nutritional profiles. Not a day goes by that a current health publication isn't touting some new food for its easily digestible, antioxidant-rich, full-spectrum nutrients. These "superfoods" range from weeds that may easily grow in your backyard to Amazonian fruits mined from the depths of the jungle. Welcome to the age of "superfoods."

I have highlighted 15 specific foods that have emerged to be truly superfoods, both medicinal and culinary. I've scoured the findings of doctors, healers, health writers, herbalists, body builders, and triathletes in an effort to provide information about some of the most nutrient-dense foods proven to increase energy and vitality, detoxify your system, boost the immune system, and slow down the aging clock. These foods can easily be added to your fermentations as brewed teas, second fermentation flavors, or recipe additives. Each of these have their own unique flavor and nutritional characteristics that will boost the nourishment of your already super-healthy, probiotic-rich fermented drinks. It is important to note that of the various superfoods I have researched,

I am only including ones that can easily be added to your homemade fermented probiotic drinks. The realm of superfoods and
super herbs is vast and fascinating. Some might argue that I am
barely scraping the surface of the incredible and healing world of
herbology and fermentation. I consider myself a lifelong learner,
and if anyone creates a new recipe involving a perceived fermenta-
tion-incompatible herb or fruit, please contact me and let me know
about it.

Gogi berries are known as the ultimate longevity fruit and are a
small, red berry native to southeast Europe and Asia. Fortunately,
they are an incredible adaptable and resilient plant and are able to
be grown in nearly any bioregion. They are an "adaptogenic" food,
meaning they invigorate and strengthen the systems of the body
while protecting our cells from stress. Goji berries are loaded with
antioxidants and they help the body increase the production of the
human growth hormone. This speeds up recovery time after sur-
gery and extreme fitness while slowing down the aging process.

They are a rich source of vitamins C, B1, B2, and B3 and more than 30 essential and trace minerals including zinc, copper, calcium, selenium, and phosphorous. This magnificent berry is also a complete protein, meaning it contains all the essential amino acids. It is also celebrated for its ability to restore sexual vigor, improve overall stamina, and contribute to a healthier, more satisfying romantic life.

Goji berries are gaining popularity and can be found in most health-food stores. They are a small red berry, typically found dried and packaged. They can be eaten as they are, sprinkled on salads, blended in smoothies, or added to kombucha, Jun, lacto-fermented teas and sodas, and kvass.

Bee pollen is considered by nutritionists to be the most complete food ever discovered. It is an alkaline-forming food that contains every known nutrient necessary to sustain human life—meaning the human species could live exclusively on bee pollen. Similar to probiotic drinks, it's a rich source of all B vitamins, including elevated levels of vitamins C, D, and E. Bee pollen is the richest source of bioavailable protein found in nature. It is 25% protein, containing all the essential amino acids. It has been used by athletes for endurance, speed, strength, muscle growth, and definition. Bee pollen is abundant in minerals and trace minerals containing barium, boron,

calcium, copper, iron, iodine, magnesium, manganese phosphorous, potassium, selenium, silicon, sulfur, sodium, and zinc.

Bee pollen is high in antioxidants, a fertility enhancer, and a potent aphrodisiac. It's usually found in granules in the refrigerated section of most health-food stores. It can also be purchased online. Bee pollen has a dry, slightly sweet, and floral flavor. It blends well in smoothies, juices, and water and can be a great addition to kombucha, water kefir, and lacto-fermented teas and sodas. In fact, commercial kombucha companies have begun bottling kombucha with honey and bee pollen. It adds an additional boost of nutrition and a sweet floral flavor.

Raw cacao comes from the beans of a pod-fruit native to central and south America and has a long history involving fermentation. Also called cocoa beans, cacao is what chocolate is made from. I am not encouraging you to go out and eat a Hershey Bar and call it health food. The cocoa beans that conventional chocolate is fashioned from are roasted at a high heat that destroys the majority of the nutritional benefits. Commercial chocolate also has refined sugar, dairy, and other chemicals. Raw chocolate is considered one of the most nutrient-dense foods ever discovered. It's particularly celebrated for its antioxidant content of which some scientists claim contains the highest amounts of antioxidants studied in any

plant. Cacao is also a good source of magnesium, iron, chromium, manganese, and zinc. This magic bean contains the natural "bliss chemical" anandamide, a cannabinoid endorphin that the human body naturally produces after exercise that makes us feel great (cacao is the only plant that this chemical has been found in).

Contributing to its mood-elevating properties, cacao contains phenylethylamine (PEA), which is a class of chemicals that we produce in our bodies when we fall in love. PEAs also play a role in increased focus and alertness. PEAs combined with the high level of magnesium makes raw cacao a natural appetite suppressant. Referred to as the "Aztec Heart Food," cacao is excellent for cardiovascular health. It contains the chemical theobromine, which dilates the cardiovascular system, making the heart's job easier.

Raw cacao has a slightly bitter flavor similar to coffee and can be found in most health-food stores. The most common ways it's found is as a powder, nibs (small, broken pieces of the bean), or as a whole bean. Cacao powder blends easily in smoothies and juices and can be used in place of cocoa or carob powder in any recipe. I enjoy adding cacao to smoothies containing coconut kefir because of how well its rich chocolatey flavor blends together with the sweet nuttiness of the fermented coconut.

Maca is considered an ancient secret of the Incans, rich in calcium, magnesium, phosphorous, potassium, sulfur, sodium, iron, and trace minerals including zinc, iodine, copper, selenium, bismuth, manganese, tin, and silicon. Similar to goji berries, maca is an adaptogen. It increases the body's power of resistance against multiple stressors, including physical, chemical, and biological agents. It contains immune-enhancing sterols, including sitosterol, campesterol, ergosterol, brassicasterol, and ergostadienol. Nowadays, it's commonly used by competitive athletes due to its ability to increase energy, stamina, oxygen in the blood, physical strength, and neurotransmitter production.

Maca is most commonly known for its libido-enhancing properties. It does not contain any hormones; however, it can be used as a hormone-replacement food. It jogs the pituitary gland into producing the precursor hormones that ultimately end up raising

estrogen, progesterone, and testosterone levels as well as balancing the thyroid, hypothalamus, pancreas, and adrenals. It is maca's ability to regulate and support the endocrine system that makes it such an excellent cure for chronic fatigue, depression, stress, tension, and adrenal exhaustion.

Maca can be found in most health-food stores. It is most commonly found dried and ground to a powder. Maca's flavor is light, nutty, and malty. It can be easily blended in smoothies, juices, or water. I enjoy combining maca with cacao, coconut milk, and any dairy or coconut milk-based kefir fermentation. Maca goes particularly well with peach and mango kefir.

Spirulina belongs to a class of single-celled blue-green spiral algae. Spirulina is 65 to 71% protein, making it the highest concentration of protein found in any food ever discovered. It is a complete protein source containing all nine essential amino acids and is celebrated for its importance in balancing brain chemistry. It is rich in vitamins A, B1, B2, B6, E, and K and an abundant natural source of chlorophyll. Chlorophyll is an essential blood builder and blood purifier. It also contains as much iron as red meat and is one of the best sources of gamma-linoleic acid (GLA), an anti-inflammatory essential fatty acid necessary for a healthy nervous system.

Spirulina has a very earthy, green, and sea vegetable flavor to it. It can be found in most health-food stores or online in tablets, capsules, or powdered form. Spirulina can be blended with very sweet fruit smoothies and fruit juices. Similar to bee pollen, spirulina can be added at the end of a fermentation before bottling.

Coconut is a hearty, tropical nut consisting of more than 90% raw saturated fat—an important building block of every cell in the human body. Consuming coconuts improves digestion and absorption of fat-soluble vitamins and amino acids. Coconuts are valuable to the immune system because they contain healthy antiviral, antimicrobial saturated fatty acids that help fight off viruses, bacteria,

and fungal growth. They improve the utilization of blood sugar and they improve the absorption of calcium and magnesium. Coconuts increase the speed and function of the thyroid, which make them great for your metabolism. They also help the body efficiently use the essential fatty acids omega-3, -6, and -9.

Young coconuts contain a nourishing liquid called "coconut water," which we use in this book for the coconut water kefir recipes. Coconut water is nature's sports drink and is packed with electrolytes, which are great for hydration. It is considered an excellent nutrition source for infants and children because it contains organic compounds that promote muscle size and general physical health. Coconut water can also be used as a topical for rashes and skin eruptions.

If you live in a tropical region, coconuts can be found everywhere. They are a resilient nut that can float in the sea for hundreds of miles, land on a beach, and grow a tree. They can also be found in many grocery stores in the shell, dried, or as coconut oil and coconut butter. In the kefir section of this book, we use blended coconut milk both for its delicious, creamy flavor as well as for its superfood nutrition.

Chia seeds are tiny but offer a massive amount of nutrition for both the body and the brain. They were celebrated as an energy food

among the ancient Aztecs and Mayans. Chia seeds are packed with protein, omega-3s, healthy fats, calcium, manganese, magnesium, and phosphorus. Nearly all the carbohydrates in chia seeds are fiber. This makes them very hydrophilic, meaning that they can absorb 10 to 12 times their weight in water. Consuming them helps keep your body hydrated. The ratios of fat, carbohydrates, and protein combined with their ability to mega hydrate, making them a great food for weight-loss and a fitness superfood.

Chia seeds are very small and can be blended with fruit smoothies, fruit juices, and water. When combined with liquid, they create a pleasant mucilaginous texture similar to tapioca. Being a vegetarian, I included chia seeds in my diet regularly as a protein source. When making fermentations, I like to add them to my kombucha, Jun, lacto-fermented sodas, and Fruit Kvass just before bottling them. Usually 1 tablespoon per 16-ounce bottle works well. You can certainly include more, but your probiotic drink will become more of a gel than a drink.

Cayenne pepper is a popular spice severely under-recognized as a medicinal food . . . perhaps because it is looked over by everyone

who doesn't care for spicy cuisine. Cayenne pepper aids in normalizing blood pressure, which makes it an excellent cardiovascular food. It is also is high in vitamin A, vitamin C, vitamin E, vitamin B6, vitamin K, manganese, and potassium. Capsaicin, the medicinal ingredients in cayenne pepper, is a potent pain reliever, metabolism booster, and appetite suppressant, which makes cayenne pepper a great dieting food.

Cayenne pepper can be purchased fresh at your grocery or dried in flakes or powder form. It can also be purchased and consumed in capsule form. Cayenne pepper mixes well in water, juice, and smoothies. I start my morning off every day with 16 ounces of warm water with the juice of half of a lemon and ½ teaspoon of cayenne pepper. I enjoy flavoring my fermentations with cayenne pepper by combing it with flavors such as ginger, lemon, goji berry, cinnamon, and cacao (see the Goji Ginger Cayenne Kombucha recipe, page 48).

Tulsi or holy basil: Tulsi is a an adaptogen, with anti-inflammatory and antioxidant properties. Apoptogenic plants (maca and goji berries are in this category, as well) help the body manage and adapt to stress. This includes chemical, physical, infectious, and emotional stress. Tulsi also has an impressive nutritional profile containing vitamins A and C, calcium, zinc, iron, and chlorophyll. It has been

used to treat people with arthritis, fibromyalgia, depression, and anxiety. Tulsi can be taken in capsule, powder, or tea form.

One of the most popular ways that people enjoy tulsi is as an herbal "tea" or tisane. To make tulsi tea, boil 1 cup of purified water and pour it over 1 teaspoon of fresh or dried tulsi leaves. Ideally, if you are using dried or powdered tulsi, you would use ½ teaspoon. Cover the water and allow to steep for 10 minutes or longer. Strain out the leaves, sweeten if necessary, and enjoy.

In Ayurveda, tulsi tea is highly regarded for being able to bring the body into a calming state similar to yoga. Ayurveda practitioners recommend drinking it daily to foster clear thoughts, relaxation, and an overall sense of well-being. In the kombucha chapter, I talked about making herbal teas where you combine half black or green tea and half medicinal herbs of your choosing. Tulsi can be enjoyed this way to make a more medicinal, calming, and stress-relieving kombucha. It also can be used to make medicinal lacto-fermented teas as discussed in chapter 6. You can add tulsi to any of your secondary ferments for a nutritional boost and to enjoy its therapeutic properties. Since it's related to the culinary basil family, it tastes slightly floral with hints of pepper and lemon. Ultimately, it doesn't have an offensive flavor and goes well with most infusions and flavorings.

Kava may also be referred to as kava kava. It's a plant native to the South Pacific islands that has been used for hundreds of years as a ceremonial health drink to promote a state of relaxation. Kava contains an active ingredient called kavalactones, believed to affect neurotransmitters in the brain and help reduce stress, alleviate anxiety, and aid in sleep. Kava was originally consumed as a liquid after the roots were ground to a paste and mixed with water (originally this grinding was done by chewing the roots and spitting them out). Nowadays, kava can be taken in tea, capsule, powder, or liquid form. Kava tea is the most common way to consume kava for anxiety, insomnia, or just to enjoy the relaxing benefits of it. When purchasing kava tea, it's important to find one that lists the kavalactone content and any other ingredients. Avoid anything that says "proprietary blends," which could mean unknown

additional additives resulting in not knowing how much actual kava you're getting. Kava tea is one of the preferred teas from the health specialists at MKE Mind Body Wellness, who use it to make lacto-fermented teas, as we discussed in chapter 6. Similar to tulsi, it can be brewed alongside green tea and black tea to make a medicinal kombucha.

Medium-grind Kava root is the most traditional type you can buy. The root is ground similar to coffee. You can brew it just like normal tea. The traditional method is done by kneading it and straining it through a muslin cloth after steeping it in hot water. Many people don't like the flavor of kava: it has an earthy taste and, as an herbal tea, it has been compared to tasting like "muddy water." Kava can be added to your fruit-based ferments, specifically second fermentations, to mask the unpleasant flavor.

Ginger is a versatile, delicious, and medicinal spice that is included in many foods around the world as well as quite a few of the fermentation recipes in this book. If you haven't already discovered it, ginger is a root loaded with nutrients and bioactive compounds that have powerful benefits to our brains and body. Gingerol is the main bioactive compound that gives ginger its anti-inflammatory and antioxidant effects. The anti-inflammatory properties make ginger a great reliever of muscle and joint pain. In addition, it's

known to drastically lower blood sugar, boost the immune system, relieve nausea, and treat chronic indigestion.

Ginger can be purchased as whole, fresh root, and in powder, tea, or capsule form. A very easy way to consume ginger is by making a tea or preparing delicious food with it. Ginger is a popular spice in Indian, Chinese, Korean, Thai, and many other international cuisines. It can be made sweet, as in the case with gingersnap cookies, or savory, as in spicy coconut curries. It's also a popular flavoring agent in sodas, nonalcoholic brews, and cocktails.

Yerba maté is an herbal tisane usually enjoyed as a tea brewed from the leaves of an evergreen holly tree native to the South American rainforest. It makes a strong and slightly bitter hot herbal beverage similar to green tea. It's very popular in Argentina and is increasing in popularity throughout the world, but not because of how it tastes—because of how it makes you feel. Similar to green tea, it's loaded with antioxidants: 5.5 times higher than green tea with a

ORAC value of 11,000. Yerba maté contains seven out of nine essential amino acids and nearly every vitamin and mineral your body needs. It's slightly caffeinated and provides a smooth, non-jittery boost in physical energy. It also provides an alert wakefulness and improves mental focus.

Yerba maté is usually consumed as a tea that can be brewed with 1 teaspoon per 8 ounces of hot water. Traditionally in South America where it is much more popular, people drink it in a gourd called a calabash, sipping through a metal straw with a filter at the end. Similar to tulsi or kava, yerba maté can be brewed alongside green tea and black tea to make a medicinal kombucha. Yerba maté can be enjoyed this way to make a more medicinal and nutritious kombucha. It also can be used to make medicinal lacto-fermented teas as discussed in chapter 6. You can add yerba maté to any of your secondary ferments for a nutritional boost and to enjoy its therapeutic properties. Yerba maté has a flavor similar to a strong green tea but slightly more bitter. It does not have an offensive flavor, and for those who enjoy it, it goes well with most infusions and flavorings.

Echinacea is a purple coneflower that has been used worldwide for boosting the immune system and treating such ailments as the common cold and the flu. What many are not aware of is that in addition to being a super immunity booster, echinacea is loaded with antioxidants that protect the body against oxidative stress. Some of these known antioxidants are flavonoids, cichoric acid, and rosmarinic acid. These same flavonoids and phytonutrients are highly anti-inflammatory, promoting healing and significantly reducing chronic pain and swelling. In addition to improving immunity and lowering inflammation, echinacea is known to lower blood sugar, reduce anxiety, and have anti-cancer properties. Echinacea is as healthy for the human body inside as it is outside. Echinacea extract is very common in skin-care products due to its impressive ability to improve skin hydration and reduce wrinkles. It also can be used to treat eczema and acne.

Of the nine species of this flower, only three are used in herbal supplements. The roots, leaves, and flowers are all used medicinally. For the sake of the recipes in this book, I suggest making echinacea tisane, which is made by brewing the leaves and flowers. The suggested quantity for making echinacea tea is ¼ cup of loose, dried echinacea leaves and flowers per 8 ounces of hot water. Allow it to steep for 10 to 15 minutes to extract the nutrition and health properties.

Echinacea tisane is not considered a tasty herbal drink. It is usually packaged as an herbal tea with other more complementary flavors such as lemongrass, peppermint, or ginger. Since echinacea is commonly taken to boost the immune system when someone has a common cold, I like combining it with sinus-clearing herbs like ginger, cayenne, and lemongrass. It goes particularly well with the Goji Ginger Cayenne Kombucha recipe on page 48. Echinacea is a wonderful herbal addition to your green and black teas when brewing your kombucha for the added medicinal benefits. It also can be added later for second fermentation or to make lacto-fermented teas as discussed in chapter 6.

Aloe vera is a thick, short-stemmed plant that stores an abundance of hydration in its leaves. Aloe is arguably more popular in the cosmetic industry than in the food industry, but its recognition globally for being an internal healer is rapidly growing among supplement and pharmaceutical companies. Aloe leaves are full of a slimy tissue similar to a "gel," which is where all of its super bioactive plant compounds are found. It is full of antioxidants, vitamins, minerals, and amino acids. The variety of antioxidant found in aloe vera, called polyphenols, are also known to have antibacterial properties that inhibit the growth of harmful bacteria that can cause infections in humans. Aloe vera is a powerful internal as

well as external healer. It is widely used to treat burns and accelerate healing of the skin on the outside. When taken internally, aloe vera is known to treat ulcers and inflammatory bowel conditions. It also can be consumed internally as well as applied externally to improve skin health and reduce wrinkles. In addition to its unique therapeutic properties for healing skin and tissue, aloe vera can be used to reduce dental plaque, treat canker sores, reduce constipation, and lower blood sugar.

Aloe vera can be purchased fresh in your grocery store, health-food store, or online as a gel, juice, supplement, oil, or powder. Aloe vera in all its forms can be easily added to any of the smoothie recipes found in chapter 4 or chapter 6. When it is purchased fresh, as a juice or a gel, it has a slimy texture and unpleasant, bitter taste. Aloe vera can be added to any of your second ferments for the additional nutritional boost, but I wouldn't suggest using it for additional flavor. One of the interesting things about the natural microbiology of aloe vera is that if you buy 100% aloe vera juice, which is actually more of a liquid gel, it will begin to ferment naturally in your refrigerator by day 7, creating an effervescent, fermented probiotic drink. I have found that the slimy texture of this superfood does not usually complement the viscosity of my fermentations, so I eat it plain or just blend it up with my kefir-based smoothies.

Turmeric is a yellow-orange root sometimes sold and labeled as yellow ginger even though it tastes nothing like ginger. Turmeric, a superfood, is arguably one of the most common and effective nutritional supplements for the brain and body. It has been used in India for thousands of years as a spice and medicinal herb. It is the spice that gives curry seasoning its color.

Only recently have scientists and western medical doctors discovered that what makes turmeric so special is a series of plant compounds called curcuminoids, the most popular of which is curcumin. Curcumin has powerful anti-inflammatory effects and is a very strong antioxidant. Curcumin is a bioactive substance that fights inflammation at the molecular cellular level. In addition to containing powerful antioxidants, curcumin boosts the activity of the body's own antioxidant enzymes, meaning it neutralizes free

radicals on its own, but also stimulates the body's ability for anti-oxidant defenses. This double combination of super antioxidants and anti-inflammatory compounds is why curcumin has made a name for itself preventing and treating Alzheimer's disease. It is known that inflammation and oxidative damage play a major role in Alzheimer's disease, and curcumin has a beneficial effect on both.

Another reason turmeric is such a super brain food is that curcumin boosts Brain-Derived Neuropathic Factor (BDNF), which is a type of growth hormone that functions in the brain. In addition to being an effective treatment of Alzheimer's, curcumin's ability to increase BDNF levels have been shown to be very effective on depression as well as improved memory. Curcumin has also been shown to lower risk of heart disease, prevent cancer, and treat a variety of inflammatory conditions such as arthritis.

Turmeric can be purchased as a whole fresh root, dried, powdered, or in capsules. Compared to ginger, turmeric's taste is mild. It is not off-putting, but it also doesn't stand out as incredibly delicious. In cooking, turmeric is used more for color than flavor. Fresh or dried turmeric can be used to make a tisane, which can go well with creating medicinal kombucha, colorful second ferments, or as an agent in creating bright yellow and medicinal lacto-fermented teas. I enjoy using turmeric as one of many auxiliary ingredients in making kvass. It is a nice addition to the Orange Carrot Kvass recipe found on page 161. Turmeric also blends well in any smoothie. Nearly every morning, my breakfast consists of a smoothie made with fermented ingredients and I make sure to always throw in a fresh piece of turmeric and a fresh piece of ginger.

Resources

Books

Delicious Probiotic Drinks: 75 Recipes for Kombucha, Kefir Ginger Beer, and Other Naturally Fermented Drinks by Julia Mueller

Kombucha: Healthy Beverage and Natural Remedy from the Far East, Its Correct Preparation and Use by Gunther W. Frank

Kombucha, Kefir and Beyond by Alex Lewin and Raquel Guajardo

Kombucha Revolution: 75 Recipes for Homemade Brews, Fixers, Elixirs and Mixers by Stephen Lee and Ken Koopman

Probiotics for Health: 100 Amazing and Unexpected uses for Probiotics by Jo A. Panyko

Superfoods for Life, Cultured and Fermented Beverages by Meg Thompson

The Art of Fermentation by Sandor Ellix Katz

The Big Book of Kombucha: Brewing, Flavoring, and Enjoying the Health Benefits of Fermented Tea by Alex LaGory and Hannah Crum

The Probiotic Cure by Martie Whittekin

True Brews: How to Craft Fermented Cider, Beer, Wine, Sake, Soda, Mead, Kefir and Kombucha at Home by Emma Christensen

Wild Fermentation: The Flavor, Nutrition and Craft of Live-Cultured Foods by Sandor Ellix Katz

Websites

Cultures for Health: This is a terrific website that offers recipes, video tutorials, DIY kitchen equipment, and starter cultures. www.culturesforhealth.com

Cultured Food Life: This is a great educational site that divides its material into 4 categories: kombucha, kefir, cultured vegetables, and sourdough/sprouted breads. It is loaded with content, which includes, articles, recipes, a podcast, books, starter cultures, and both free and paid courses and workshops. www.culturedfoodlife.com

Fermented Food Lab: This exclusively an education site run by fermentation educator Danielle Ramirez. What I like about this site is that it is easily accessible, geared toward beginners, and there is an abundant of free courses and workshops as well as paid ones. www.fermentedfoodlab.com

Ferment Works: This site is the home-base and education center of fermentation teachers Kirsten and Christopher Shockey. They are a husband and wife duo who have written multiple books on fermentation, including one of my favorites, *Fiery Ferments: Hot Sauces, Spicy Chutneys, Kimchis with Kick.* www.ferment.works

Fermentation on Wheels: This is a traveling education hub whose goal it is to bridge communities by teaching fermentation and sustainability. This website offers books, recipes, resources, and events for fellow fermentation enthusiasts. www.fermentationonwheels.com

Kombucha Kamp: This website is specific to kombucha and kefir and is run by kombucha pioneer and expert fermenter Hannah Crum. It serves as an excellent educational resource for brewing your own kombucha as well as a one-stop shop for purchasing quality kitchen fermentation tools. www.kombuchakamp.com

Mastering Fermentation: This website is a very dense fermentation educational resource center and ecommerce site run by author, cooking teacher, and master fermenter Mary Karlin. She offers recommended reading, downloadable fermentation charts, kitchen tools, and online video lessons www.masteringfermentation.com

The Cultured Club: This amazing website is a gathering place for people who like to ferment, eat, learn, listen, and share information regarding the way our gut health shapes our overall well-being.

Here you can also purchase the very helpful recipe book called *The Cultured Club: Fabulous Fermentation Recipes.*
www.theculturedclub.com

Wild Fermentation: This website is the blog and resource center of famous author and fermentation educator Sandoor Ellix Katz. Here you can purchase books on fermentation, learn about fermentation events around the world, shop, and chat with other fermentation enthusiasts on a fermentation support forum.
www.wildfermentation.com

Acknowledgments

I WOULD LIKE TO THANK Stacy Tornio for lighting the fire for this book and helping me discover what I am capable of. A HUGE tearful thank-you to my editor, Nicole Frail, for all of her hard work, patience, and guidance for a first-time author. Thank you to my loving and supportive family. I have wonderful parents and two inspiring sisters who comprise an unassuming gang of amateur fermenters, kitchen scientists, organic gardeners, creative thinkers, and health renegades. I am the person I am today because of each of you.

Index

Conversion Charts

Metric and Imperial Conversions

(These conversions are rounded for convenience)

Ingredient	Cups/ Tablespoons/ Teaspoons	Ounces	Grams/ Milliliters
Fruit, dried	1 cup	4 ounces	120 grams
Fruits or veggies, chopped	1 cup	5 to 7 ounces	145 to 200 grams
Fruits or veggies, puréed	1 cup	8.5 ounces	245 grams
Honey, maple syrup, or corn syrup	1 tablespoon	0.75 ounce	20 grams
Liquids: cream, milk, water, or juice	1 cup	8 fluid ounces	240 milliliters
Salt	1 teaspoon	0.2 ounces	6 grams
Spices: cinnamon, cloves, ginger, or nutmeg (ground)	1 teaspoon	0.2 ounce	5 milliliters
Sugar, brown, firmly packed	1 cup	7 ounces	200 grams
Sugar, white	1 cup/ 1 tablespoon	7 ounces/0.5 ounce	200 grams/12.5 grams
Vanilla extract	1 teaspoon	0.2 ounce	4 grams

Liquids

8 fluid ounces = 1 cup = ½ pint
16 fluid ounces = 2 cups = 1 pint
32 fluid ounces = 4 cups = 1 quart
128 fluid ounces = 16 cups = 1 gallon